THE
G · I · F · T
of
Angels

THE
G·I·F·T
of
Angels

RACHEL ANN
NUNES

BONNEVILLE BOOKS
AN IMPRINT OF CEDAR FORT, INC.
SPRINGVILLE, UTAH

This is a work of fiction. The characters, names, incidents, places, and dialogue are products of the author's imagination, and are not to be construed as real. The opinions and views expressed herein belong solely to the author and do not necessarily represent the opinions or views of Cedar Fort, Inc. Permission for the use of sources, graphics, and photos is also solely the responsibility of the author.

ISBN 13: 978-1-4621-1112-1

Published by Bonneville Books, an imprint of Cedar Fort, Inc., 2373 W. 700 S., Springville, UT 84663
Distributed by Cedar Fort, Inc., www.cedarfort.com

LIBRARY OF CONGRESS CATALOGING-IN-PUBLICATION DATA

Nunes, Rachel Ann, 1966- author.
 The gift of angels / Rachel Ann Nunes.
   pages cm
 Summary: Angela Thornberry, stricken with cancer, wonders why people all around her talk about miracles happening to them when the one she needs doesn't seem to be happening to her.
 ISBN 978-1-4621-1112-1 (alk. paper)
 1. Mormon women--Fiction. 2. Cancer--Patients--Fiction. I. Title.

 PS3564.U468G44 2012
 813'.54--dc23

2012015654

Cover design by Angela D. Olsen
Cover design © 2012 by Lyle Mortimer
Edited and typeset by Kelley Konzak

Printed in the United States of America

10 9 8 7 6 5 4 3 2 1

Printed on acid-free paper

To all the angels who have touched my life.

BOOKS BY RACHEL ANN NUNES

**Autumn Rain Novels
(Paranormal Romance)**
Imprints
Shades of Gray
Final Call
Line of Fire

Romantic Suspense
*Eyes of a Stranger (Autumn
Rain Series Prequel)*
Tell Me No Lies

Women's Fiction
Flying Home
Fields of Home
Saving Madeline
Before I Say Goodbye
A Greater Love
A Heartbeat Away

Huntington Family
Winter Fire
No Longer Strangers
Chasing Yesterday
By Morning Light
The Independence Club

Ariana Series
Ariana: The Making of a Queen
Ariana: A Gift Most Precious

Ariana: A New Beginning
Ariana: A Glimpse of Eternity
This Time Forever
Ties That Bind
Twice in a Lifetime

**Love Series
(Romantic Suspense)**
A Bid for Love
Framed for Love
Love on the Run

Romance
To Love and to Promise
Tomorrow and Always
Bridge to Forever
Where I Belong
A Greater Love
This Very Moment
In Your Place (Young Adult)

For Children
*The Problem with Spaceships:
Zero G*
Daughter of a King
The Secret of the King

Acknowledgments

Thanks to Lyle Mortimer and the great folks at Cedar Fort, especially Jennifer Fielding for her patience with this project above and beyond the call of duty, Kelley Konzak for making me look better with her editing, Angela Olsen for a beautiful cover, and the marketing team for their efforts to get the book into readers' hands. Thanks everyone!

Appreciation also goes to my supportive family for their encouragement with this "fictional nonfiction novella." And a huge thanks to pre-reader Julie Bellon, who told me that *The Gift of Angels* might just be the best gospel-oriented book I've ever written. I think her exact words were, "I didn't know you had this in you." Thanks, Julie! Though you may not have realized it, your faith helped me see this story through to publication.

One

I sat in church near the back, feeling I might shatter into a million pieces no one would ever be able to put back together. My hands tightened on the edge of the padded bench to prevent me from standing up and screaming until everyone stared, especially the speaker. I wanted him to stop talking about miracles and angels, because they don't happen to everyone—just to a lucky few. I'd already learned that much. For me, angels do not exist.

"So I prayed," my neighbor droned on from the pulpit. "I prayed, and that was when I felt . . ."

Who cared how God miraculously healed his latest infection? I wanted my neighbor—wanted them all—to weep with me . . . for me.

I wanted to know why I'd never been able to find a miracle in my life. Why God didn't send me an angel when I needed one the most.

I stood, my muscles so taut they ached.

My husband, Dean, looked at me. "Are you okay?" he mouthed.

I nodded, keeping my face blank.

He blinked once, his expression all too clear. He understood and would excuse me yet again to our daughter or any curious friends.

Not that anyone would really miss me. Even Dean would be occupied teaching his youth Sunday School class, trying to get in a few words through the babble of self-centered teenage voices. Our fourteen-year-old daughter, Marie, was in his class.

I pushed past Marie—one of our two children left at home—glad that our son Brody was at his friend's missionary farewell today so I didn't have to endure the question in his eyes. Marie didn't meet my gaze but frowned as my shoe hit the edge of the scriptures she'd placed on the carpet in front of her chair.

Look at me! I wanted to shout. *Feel for me!*

I bit my lip, seeing for a brief, frozen moment in time a vision of Marie as a baby. I remembered how much she'd needed me, how much she'd loved me, and though I was happily past that stage in my life, I suddenly longed for the feel of her newborn self against my chest. I craved the touch of her once-chubby arms around my neck. The amazing, clean baby smell.

Now she was nearly grown, and I was invisible to her.

In my car, a new Mazda, I drove away. Fast. Too fast. The roar of the engine gave me the feeling of power, the manual transmission a sense of control.

A false sense of control, as it turned out. There was nothing I could control in my life now.

I wanted to turn on the music, to feel it beating over me, drowning out my grief—and yes, my anger. But I didn't listen to non-church music on Sundays and couldn't quite bring myself to do it even now. Why I still adhered to that standard was beyond me. What had being good done for me? What had obeying any of the commandments accomplished? Everything I thought I'd been given in return would soon be ripped away. Even my family.

Instead of blasting the music, I opened the window and let the cool April air beat in on me, sending my brown hair flying so erratically that it almost obscured my vision. The cold made me feel more alive.

Time passed.

After I'd been on the freeway for what seemed like hours, I turned off at an abandoned-looking exit and killed the engine, not recognizing the area where my car had come to rest. I sat, still gripping the wheel, my heart pounding and tears coursing down my cheeks.

I'm lost, I thought. *I'm lost, but I know I don't want to ever go home.*

I wasn't thinking about the home I shared with Dean and our children.

My scriptures were on the passenger seat where I had thrown them, closed as they had been since my diagnosis last month. I hadn't been able to open them. I felt too betrayed.

Life was now divided into two parts: before and after. Before, everything had hope and promise. After, there was only sadness and death. One single moment had changed my life forever. Before, I hadn't really known that such a thing was possible. Surely there first had to be signs, warning, hints, some fault to be placed—anything but this pointless, catastrophic instant that greedily consumed even the tiniest ray of hope.

Before that instant, I'd begun reading the Bible again, planning to go from start to finish as I hadn't done since my early wifehood. Waiting for my daughter when I picked her up from play practice provided a perfect opportunity. At first it had taken effort to make myself read, but soon I'd been swept up in the magic of the words. I'd always loved Bible scriptures as a child.

After the terrible instant, I couldn't make myself open the book. I almost felt I couldn't touch it without searing my hands.

I touched it now, closing my eyes against the pain, real and imagined. The tears continued to wet my face, my hands, the scriptures—anywhere they fell. I wondered if there would always be more tears. If it was possible to drown in tears.

Where was my faith? Why did I feel so abandoned? All I wanted was a little miracle. Something that would be so utterly simple for the God I believed in. Was that too much to ask?

Apparently.

The specialist had confirmed my general practitioner's diagnosis, and I was to start chemotherapy on Tuesday, followed by radiation and hopefully surgery, which would then be followed by more treatments. It was now the beginning of April, and if there was no surgery, they didn't hold much hope that I would see the leaves turn color. Even if they got me to a point where I could have the surgery, the oh-so-slim survival rate was not something to celebrate.

I held the scriptures until the furious beating of my heart slowed to a tolerable pace. With effort, I opened the Bible to where I'd been reading in Genesis. I hadn't delved far into the book, since I'd been looking up all the cross-references and even taking notes. I didn't remember any of it now. I decided to scan the chapter headings to recall where the story had been leading.

The text swam before my eyes, but I focused enough to see that Abraham and his wife Sarah were being promised a child in their old age. I turned several more pages, unwilling to hear about another miracle. Finally, I started reading again, and though it was more of the same story, I couldn't look away. The words took control of my imagination.

I held in my hand not scriptures, but a pitcher of water. I wore a natural-color dress that I suspected was made of wool, my head covered by a similar fabric that shielded me from the hot sun overhead. Before me stood a black, goat-hair tent surrounded by others of the same color. A group of children squatted between two of these structures, playing in the sand. An old woman sat in the shade near them, her large, capable hands sewing a seam on a stretch of the same black tent material.

In the settlement, I could see a group of men, a few animals, women at a well. Beyond that, nothing but endless dirt and sand, broken only by an occasional acacia tree.

An old man emerged from the tent, his weathered face slick with tears. I bent my head quickly and went inside.

I found a woman there, sitting on a mound of blankets and cuddling a newborn at her breast. Like the man, her wrinkled face was wet with tears, but her countenance was illuminated, as if her joy was too great to be contained in her aged frame. Work-worn hands smoothed the baby's soft cheek.

I poured water into a bowl near the woman's bed. She reached out and touched my hand in thanks.

Then she laughed.

Startled, I began to ask a question, but she spoke first. "God hath made me to laugh, so that all that hear will laugh with me. Who would have said under Abraham that Sarah should have given children suck? For I have born him a son in his old age."

The scene before me disappeared, and I was back in my car, wondering what had happened. I'd always tried to immerse myself in the scriptures, but never before had it been quite like this, as though I'd actually been there.

A child. Hope for the future. A miracle for Sarah and Abraham. My shoulders convulsed with a sob, and I slammed the scriptures shut.

At first I'd actually thought I might be pregnant again after all these years. The early symptoms of nausea, abdominal discomfort, and lack of energy had been much the same as I remembered while expecting each of my seven children. At forty-eight, the idea of another baby was shocking, but not exactly unwelcome. I was at a transition time anyway, with my oldest five, three boys and two girls, married and well on their way in life, and my younger son soon graduating from high school next month. Not even Marie really needed me—except to drive her everywhere.

I'd always kept busy and lately had begun to toy with the idea of opening my own restaurant. A baby would have sent me in another direction altogether but not necessarily a bad one. That I wasn't pregnant was my first clue something was horribly, horribly wrong. The human body suddenly seemed too fragile for words.

Dean had come with me to all the doctor appointments after that first terrifying one where an ultrasound had shown a mass on my pancreas, and his support had been the only reason I hadn't completely given up. We hadn't told any of the children yet.

I bit my lip so hard I tasted blood.

If the worst happened, the older children would be all right, but I still worried about Marie. Despite her apparent independence, surely there was still much I needed to teach her. The more she pushed me away, the more I wanted to cling to her.

Only last week I'd gone with her ninth-grade drama class on a field trip to see a play. I had been expecting a pleasant morning of conversation and joking around with her and her friends. But Marie had sat far back in the bus, crammed into a seat with two other girls, giggling and laughing. She ignored me completely.

Suddenly I'd felt as if I were back in my high school math class, where I'd never excelled, though more from lack of encouragement than lack of skill. Back to the day when a boy had thrown a gooey spit wad that had slammed into the back of my neck, entwining with my long hair.

"Ha!" someone had shouted. Giggles burst through the teacher's lecture.

Humiliated, I'd grabbed my books and run from the class, catching only a glimpse of the teacher's puzzled stare.

On the field trip with my daughter, there'd been nowhere to run. Not only was the door to the bus closed, but I was also an adult. I wasn't supposed to care about the rude actions of others, and normally I didn't. But it hurt that my own daughter didn't want to acknowledge I was her mother.

None of my other children had been that way. I'd gone on numerous field trips with them, and they'd each sat happily by me, chatting away, glad for the time together. Their friends had never minded my presence. I was a hip sort of parent, and they liked me.

Marie's friends never had a chance to like me. I was firmly excluded from their circle—by her design, not theirs.

Please, Marie, I'd wanted to turn and plead with her on the bus. *Think about what you're doing. There may not be much time left. Someday when you're finally past this selfish stage of your life, you'll regret this day. Please, honey. I love you too much to want you to carry that kind of burden.*

I knew regret. I remember leaving my mother sleeping that last day she was alive. I'd felt annoyed and slightly disgusted that she was in the depths of yet another bout of depression when I had so much good going on in my life. The high school play began that day, our debut for the other students. I didn't always want her around, of course, but that day I'd wanted her to cheer for me.

"Mom, please wake up! Aren't you coming to my play?"

She mumbled something and fell back to sleep.

"You always do this!" I slammed out of the house, angry, squealing my tires a little as I left, in case she could hear, which I doubted. It probably just annoyed the neighbors.

When my dad finally found me after school at my friend's house, it was to tell me she was dead.

Oh, yes, I knew regrets, and I knew all about what-ifs.

The adult me knew it wasn't my fault. There'd been too many times when my mother had slept away the day, dealing with her depression. I couldn't have known her heart was stopping, that she was dying. If I had, I would have saved her . . . somehow. I certainly wouldn't have left her lying there all alone.

I didn't want my daughter to live with that kind of regret. I didn't want one of the last vivid memories of her childhood to be of me looking back at her from the middle of the bus, my eyes begging for acknowledgment.

Why hadn't I stayed with my mother?

I could have used an angel that day to tell me to stay home. But there had been no angel for me then, and there was none for me now. I alone would have to tell my daughter the secret I was holding inside—and soon.

Two

When I arrived home, my family was clearing the table—or Dean and Brody were. Marie was poring over the Sunday comics, her straight, brown hair fanned out over her shoulders.

"Marie, put away the milk," Dean said in a voice that told me he'd already asked for her help numerous times. Our daughter slowly obeyed, taking the comics with her to read on the way to the refrigerator.

They looked up as I came farther into the room, my movements alerting them to my presence. Normally the opening of the garage would have signaled my return, but someone had left it open. No matter how I harped on my family about possible thieves, I was the only one who ever remembered to close it.

Dean smiled at me. "We've eaten, but I've saved you some." He motioned to a loaded plate of the roast, potatoes, and vegetables that I'd put in the slow cooker that morning. Of course, I couldn't possibly eat all that—nausea was my constant companion these days—but Dean tried his best to keep me from losing more weight.

"Let me warm it up a bit in the microwave first."

"Thanks," I said, not wanting to worry him. All I really wanted was to go to bed, though I probably wouldn't sleep. Mostly I was so angry, my thoughts so volatile, that at night I ended up staring at the ceiling or into the darkness for hours on end. Even so, I'd take anger any day over the shocked disbelief of the early days when I was so numb I couldn't even feel my fingers.

"How'd it go at John's ward?" I asked Brody.

Brody set a plate down by the dishwasher, his handsome face becoming animated. "His talk was really cool. He didn't even seem nervous, and a ton of people were there."

"I thought you were going to his house afterward."

"I did for a bit, but his whole family's there now, and he's sort of busy. The guys and I decided to go over later to give him the stuff we got for him. I can't believe he's going to be gone for two years."

"It'll go fast," Dean said. "Too fast. You'll see."

I swallowed tightly, feeling ill. Time was passing too fast.

"We waited for you to read scriptures," Brody said to me. "We ate first instead."

I smiled at my son and nodded, though woodenly. While I hadn't been opening my personal scriptures, Dean had taken the opposite course, making sure our family had its daily dose no matter what. He'd been sharing his book with me, not willing to ask me in front of the children to get my own. I was surprised he hadn't brought it up when we were alone, until I realized he was afraid of my response.

Strange that in my sickness I should become so powerful. Whatever I wanted, good or bad, Dean would not stand in my way. Normally we were a team of checks and balances, both of us able to suggest corrections when we perceived something was out of kilter. This new unbalance in our relationship unnerved me greatly.

Marie stood by the table where she had set the comics. "Can't we do scriptures later?" There was a book tucked under her arm, and I knew she was planning to hole up in her room and read the rest of the day. There had been a time when she'd always wanted to play board games or have me read to her.

"Now's better," Dean said, pouring me a glass of milk. "We're all here, and we all have time. I'd like to discuss what we've read this week, and since we're going to the planetarium tomorrow for family night, it'll be like doing the spiritual part today."

"Other families don't have two family nights," Marie retorted, plopping into her seat. "I don't know why I have to go to the planetarium anyway. It's not for *my* school class. Brody should go by himself, not drag us all along."

"Hey, it'll be fun," Brody protested. "You're just mad 'cause they won't let you take Becki."

Marie frowned. "Her parents would let her go. They're not so rigid about Mondays like you guys."

"That's beside the point." Dean's voice was tight,

and I knew he found our daughter as challenging as I did. Marie had always been a good girl, but with her new attitudes and the friends she'd taken up with, we were both concerned about the direction she was headed.

Brody went to Marie and put an arm around her shoulder. "Don't worry. I won't let you get bored. And I promise not to let loose too many strange smells." Mouth pursed, he made a long, disgusting sound.

"Eww, gross!" But Marie was laughing. Brody had a way with her. For all the growing up she'd done over the past few years, part of her was still the little girl who had worshiped him and followed him around to the point of driving him crazy. I had no doubt the two would have a fantastic time tomorrow night at the planetarium.

I wished I could stay home. Marveling at the miracle of the universe no longer appealed to me. The only miracle I wanted to hear about was the one I needed in my own life—and I wasn't going to hold my breath for that one.

Brody went to get scriptures for him and Marie, while Dean pulled his from the briefcase he always carried to church. They took turns reading aloud as I slowly ate the food Dean had retrieved from the microwave. The food smelled and tasted great, but my nausea made it difficult to chew. I had to force the fork with bits of meat into my mouth. At least eating slowly meant that I didn't have to read.

We had finished the Book of Mormon last week and were in 1 Nephi again, after having started with the introduction and the testimonies of the three witnesses and Joseph Smith. My bitterness had only increased in the reading. They'd all seen angels. Lehi had visions and also saw angels. I'd never realized there were so many angels in our religion.

Joseph and Lehi had angels while I had a biopsy confirming one of the most rapidly growing cancers that existed. I had surgery to put in a port four inches below my right collarbone, and through it I would receive chemotherapy drugs. That was no comparison to angels.

I stopped chewing at the thought, and Dean held his scriptures closer to me so I could see better.

Brody began reading verse twenty-eight in the third chapter of 1 Nephi. "'And it came to pass that Laman was angry with me, and also with my father; and also was Lemuel, for he hearkened unto the words of Laman. Wherefore Laman and Lemuel did speak many hard words unto us, their younger brothers, and they did smite us even with a rod.'" Brody shook his head. "Man, they're jerks."

"It doesn't say that," Marie teased. They laughed.

I knew what happened next. Another angel. An angel preoccupied with breaking up a sibling fight. Wouldn't that be nice? Tears stung my eyes, and I shut them, struggling to keep the emotion from my face.

I could shut my eyes, but I couldn't shut out the vivid images that came as my family continued to read.

The hills around me were rocky, filled with scrub brush and dotted with olive trees. Shouting came from a cave in front of me. I took a step and stumbled on a rock, falling to my knees. Rising, I brushed the dirt from my linen tunic and adjusted my mantel, my bracelets jingling. I stared at them in wonder.

More shouting came from the cave. I stepped inside, my heart pounding.

Two bearded men in light brown tunics and scarlet mantels were hitting two younger men with sticks. Whack! Whack! *The sound made me shudder with the obvious force of the blows.*

On the ground near their feet was an open chest that was empty save a single vase that glittered gold in the dim light.

I heard the younger men cry out a name that sounded like "Brother!"

Brother. Nephi and Sam. The light was dim, but I could feel the older brothers' frustration and fury. What might have begun as a simple proof of power was quickly escalating into something much more vicious, something the younger men might not survive.

Whack! Whack!

A shimmering column of light fell over the group. I squinted my eyes, but all I could see was brightness. "Why do ye smite your younger brother with a rod?" came a voice. "Know ye not that the Lord hath chosen him to be a ruler over you?"

The voice wasn't loud, but it pierced to the center of my heart.

"Behold," the angel continued, *"ye shall go up to Jerusalem again, and the Lord will deliver Laban into your hands."* Power filled every word, and I had to brace myself against the wall of the cave, close my eyes to the brightness.

"Are you okay, Mom?" Brody was looking at me with an expression similar to the one Dean had been wearing lately. His brow was wrinkled, his blue eyes intense. I noticed he'd shaved, though the few hairs he had hardly justified shaving at all.

"Fine," I managed. "Just thinking we could put that angel to good work here with you and Marie." The experience had felt so real, but my mind had to be playing tricks on me. I wondered if it was somehow connected to my illness.

"We don't fight," Marie said. "Not for real. We just tease." To make her point, she stuck her tongue out at her brother. He rolled his eyes, and she giggled. Dean looked on them with amusement.

I have to tell them soon, I thought. They deserved time to prepare themselves.

I felt as if I were seeing my family for the first time. Dark-haired, blue-eyed, boisterous Marie, a woman physically, but still immature in her actions and choices. She had become truly beautiful, a fact I'd missed despite the steady increase of boys calling the house.

Brody, taller than his dad now, his shock of sand-colored hair sitting on his head in disarray as though uncertain in what direction to lie. He was poised in that short, precious time before real manhood. Already he'd taken control of his life, and his choices proved he was worthy of the task.

Dean. Here my heart constricted. He couldn't really be called a handsome man, but he was definitely pleasant-looking, and the kindness in his eyes was unmistakable. I knew every curve, valley, and hill in that face, a face that telegraphed his thoughts long before he voiced them. I had caressed each unruly cowlick in his dark-blond hair. To me he was the most handsome man in the world, the most dependable, and the most loving. If he had been a bad husband, maybe that would make things easier. Maybe I wouldn't be so loath to leave.

"Angela?" Dean asked.

I jerked slightly at the sound of my name. Angela. So much like "angel." *It figures*, I thought. *Even my name betrays me.* Lately, I had become a philosopher of sorts. I guess dying does that to a person. Perhaps that explained the strange experiences I was having with the scriptures.

"I'm fine," I lied. "Go ahead." The last thing I wanted was to hear more about the angel, but anything was better than telling the news to my children. Once I did, there was no going back. Our whole future would change. For now I could almost pretend the only challenge I was facing was sending my son off on a mission at the end of the year.

I didn't hear what else they read, though I thought a lot about Nephi and his angel—his own personal angel. It simply wasn't fair.

Or was it? If the angel hadn't saved Nephi that day,

there might not have been a Book of Mormon, and many souls would have been lost. If Sarah hadn't given birth to Isaac, there would have been no Jacob or children of Israel. But the Lord had sent both a miracle.

What was my life compared to theirs? I wasn't going to be the mother of a great nation, lead my people to a promised land, or even find the cure to a previously incurable disease. It was a little too late for all of that.

Three

When my family had finished reading, Marie jumped up and came around the table, sitting down in the chair next to me, vacated by Dean who had gone to put away his briefcase. "Uh, Mom," she said, using the wheedling voice that instantly told me she wanted something.

I looked at her, my hand reaching out to smooth back her hair. She arched away from me impatiently, and I hardened my heart against the rejection.

"Becki and some of the others are going to the mall tomorrow. Can I go with her?"

"What are you going to do at the mall?"

She shrugged. "You know."

"No, I don't."

"Look at stuff."

Brody smirked. "You mean look at guys."

"No, I don't!" Marie glared at him. "We're just hanging out."

"Will there be adult supervision?"

Marie hesitated. "Becki says her mom is coming."

We both knew what that meant. No supervision.

History showed that Becki had a way of stretching the truth so Marie could be included. I'd lost track of all the times I'd ended up staying with the girls when another parent was supposed to be responsible. The last time had been at Nickelcade, where Marie was meeting her friends and one of their mothers, who would later give them all a ride home. When we arrived, no other parent was there. The place was filled with a variety of people, and enough older boys that I couldn't leave Marie unattended. So I'd sat watching my daughter and another girl play games while Becki whispered intimately with an older boy behind a row of arcade games where she thought I couldn't see. I'd dragged Marie out two hours later, leaving the other girls, whose mothers apparently didn't see any problem in leaving them there long after the appointed pick up hour.

"You could come to the mall with us," Marie said now.

"You mean I can come if I walk ten paces behind you." With the memory of the drama field trip so fresh in my mind, I couldn't help the bitterness in my voice. "Thanks but no thanks."

Brody snorted. "Yeah, Marie. You won't even sit with us at the movies."

I'd never minded that. I'd even encouraged her to sit up a row or two with her friends, but the mall, with Becki's older boyfriend sure to be there, was a different story.

Marie folded her arm atop her fantasy book. "I

wouldn't make you walk behind us. But I don't see why I can't go alone."

It wasn't that I didn't trust her so much as I felt she lacked judgment where Becki was concerned. "When you're a little older," I said, "you'll be able to go out more with your friends. Until then you'll need to hang out here. That's what we finished the basement for, remember?"

"You don't trust me," Marie wailed. "It's not fair! All the other kids get to go places."

"That's their parents' choice. We have our own family rules." Rules that had worked well enough for all the others. Rules that had kept them out of danger before it was too late.

"Yeah, Marie, what's the big deal? You know Becki's only going to meet boys anyway." Brody lurched to his feet, suddenly all gangly arms and legs, as though he'd forgotten exactly how to control his growing body. "Well, I gotta get going. Have to do some stuff before I go to John's." He disappeared in the direction of the stairs leading up to our bedrooms on the second floor.

"Please, Mom. It's only for a few hours," Marie pleaded.

"I'm sorry, honey."

"But why can't you go?"

"I don't think I'll be able to. I haven't been feeling well lately." It was as close as I had come to telling her about my sickness.

She didn't connect the dots. "Mom! You're so . . ."

Whatever I was she didn't say. I knew from experience that she would continue to plead and whine until she wore me down or I left the room. Something else she'd learned from Becki, whose mother always gave in. I decided to go on the attack. "Besides, there's also the matter of your chores."

"What? I did 'em! I always do them."

Five minutes in the family room and the downstairs bathroom—total—wasn't exactly doing her chores, but I wouldn't argue the point. "I'm talking about your room."

"My room?" Her brows gathered in an angry line above her eyes.

"You haven't cleaned it in a week. Which means you haven't done your chores. I let you go over to your friend's house on Friday, thinking you'd cleaned it, and you had everyone over here last night, but you lied about it being done."

"It only takes me five minutes. What's the big deal?" She jumped to her feet. "You're always making a big deal out of everything. I don't care if my room's clean. I like it the way it is."

"You haven't dusted in months!"

"That's because it takes me an hour to do the shelves."

"So? It takes me an hour to clean the kitchen and more hours to do the laundry. That's life. Cleaning takes time."

She wrinkled her nose. "Too much time."

"Not if you do one shelf a week. Look, it's not

healthy to leave all that dust and garbage around. You have to learn to keep your room clean, or what will you do someday with an entire house?"

Only a month ago Dean discovered that she'd been using one of her dresser drawers as a garbage can, and it had been crammed full of everything from used hygiene pads to candy wrappers. The display was unpleasant enough for him to ground her for an entire week. I always remembered because it was the same day I'd gotten the first bad news from the doctor.

"I'll hire a maid for my cleaning." Marie jutted out her chin.

I tried hard not to roll my eyes. "And pay her with what? No one has that much money starting out."

"I will."

"You're not going to the mall."

Her voice rose. "It's not fair!"

She was right about that. Life wasn't fair. Soon, she'd know that only too well.

"I just want to be with my friends. I can't believe you won't let me go. You don't even remember what it's like to be my age!"

But I did. I felt it now, as I had on the bus last week. Her words cut and pierced me as surely as any knife. "Marie," I said, "please try to understand. I care about you more than anything and that's why—"

"I don't care! You hate Becki. You don't trust me. You never treated Brody this way!"

Brody had never pushed at the rules. Brody had

chosen honest friends. Even if I said it aloud, she wouldn't understand.

Marie wasn't finished. She raised her book and shook it at me, her face flushed. I flinched at the anger in the lines of her face and body.

"You're so mean. All the other mothers—"

"Enough!" The loud voice echoed through the kitchen and adjoining family room, bringing Marie's rant up short. Dean stood in the kitchen doorway, fists clenched at his sides, his face livid. "That's enough," he repeated. "You're grounded for a week for talking to your mother that way. No Internet, no email, no phone, no friends. Nothing. And don't even think about letting your grades drop or you'll be grounded the rest of the month."

"But—"

"Enough!" Dean looked almost glowing in his defense of me. The clenched fists weren't a concern; he would never hit any of us. He rarely even became angry. "Now you will apologize to your mother and go to your room to think about this. And tomorrow your room had better be clean."

Marie's jaw worked as she glowered at us, but she didn't protest. "I'm sorry," she said, pushing the words between gritted teeth. Whirling, she headed to her room, her feet barely short of stomping up the stairs.

Dean watched her go. When he turned back to me, he was smiling, all traces of anger wiped from his face.

"You're not mad," I said.

He shrugged. "We need to keep her on her toes. She takes it more seriously when I look upset." He sat beside me and took my hand.

"She's going to have to take more responsibility," I heard myself saying.

His eyes met mine. "She can begin by treating her parents with respect."

I nodded, hating my life and everything in it. Everything, of course, except Dean and the children.

Much later, when I finally slept, I dreamed of Nephi's angel. I still couldn't see his face, but as he rebuked Nephi's brothers, somehow his voice reminded me of Dean's.

Four

On Tuesday morning my chemotherapy treatment at the Cottonwood hospital went smoothly, and though it was all new and I'd been worried, I didn't feel too much fear or pain. I simply sat in an easy chair reading while first one chemo drug and then another dripped into the new port on the right side of my chest between my collarbone and my breast. I was a little tired at first because they included an anti-nausea medicine to help my body accept the chemo drugs, and that made me want to sleep. Even so, I nearly read a whole novel in the three hours it took to get the drugs inside me. I didn't feel any different. Even my customary nausea hadn't worsened.

Other people were also receiving treatment, some alone and some accompanied by loved ones. As Dean chatted with the other patients, I learned I was the only one who had come for the first time that day. Contrary to the possibilities that I'd been forewarned about, there were no crying fits or dramatic reactions to the drugs, but an air of quiet and calm reigned. My internal storm was completely at odds with the atmosphere.

I made Dean go back to work after he drove me home. If he didn't sell houses, we wouldn't have an income, and we needed one more than ever now. We both felt fortunate to have adequate health insurance.

I couldn't eat a thing for lunch and instead went upstairs and climbed into bed, surprised that I didn't feel as tired as I'd expected. My turmoil was more emotional than physical, and I had the overpowering urge to feel sorry for myself. Giving in to the emotion, I lay there staring at the ceiling, utterly alone and depressed. I willed myself to sleep.

Sometime later, the doorbell rang and I started violently, my eyes snapping open. Focusing on the bedside clock, I saw an hour had passed—still too early for the children to come home from school. Besides, they used the door in the garage; they knew the code and I always left the door to the family room open for them in the afternoon.

I waited and heard the bell again. Then nothing. I wasn't going to answer. I didn't care who it was.

After a time of silence, I heard a door open somewhere in the house. I sat up, suddenly frightened. Had one of the kids come home from school early? I hadn't heard the telltale groan of the garage door. Sweat broke out over my body, and my nausea rushed back.

"Hello?" called a voice. "Angela? Angela, are you here? Angela!"

I sighed with relief and wiped my clammy hands on

the new jogging outfit I'd worn to the clinic. They'd told me to wear something comfortable.

"I'm up here, Shirley," I called, going out to the upstairs hallway that was open to the family room below. I leaned over the railing and saw her head poking in from the door leading to the garage. "Come on in."

At my invitation, she came the rest of the way inside—all six feet of her. Shirley Jefferson was a blonde woman my age who wore size eleven shoes and sewed many of her own clothes from homemade patterns. She'd been my visiting teacher for seven years and one of my closest friends in the ward for four. She was also one of the most beautiful women I knew. Today she had her shoulder-length hair in pigtails and was wearing an animal print pantsuit that made her look exotic.

"Sorry I didn't answer the door," I said. "I was taking a nap."

"Well, I'm sorry I barged in." She stared up at me with her large hazel eyes. "I got a little worried when no one answered, seeing that your garage door is open and your car's inside."

For a moment I stiffened, thinking Dean had told her about the treatment and asked her to check up on me, but I shrugged off the impression immediately. As much as he wanted to form a support group for me, Dean would never break my confidence. Or if he had, he would have given me warning. No, Shirley simply knew I didn't leave the garage open.

"Did you forget I was coming?" Shirley asked into

the awkward silence. That's when I noticed the copy of the *Ensign* rolled under her arm.

She came to visit teach, I thought. "Oh, that's right. It's the first Tuesday of the month, isn't it? I guess it did kind of slip my mind. I'll be right down."

"You sure? I could come back a little later."

I felt a strange panic that she might leave me alone to stare up at the ceiling again. "No it's fine. That would be too much work. I'll just be a minute."

I took a peek in the bathroom on my way down to make sure smeared makeup wouldn't give me away.

When I got to the family room, Shirley was sitting on my couch searching through her *Ensign*. "I didn't have a chance to read the lesson," she said apologetically. "Jan was supposed to give it."

"Where *is* Jan?" I asked, settling into my rocker with my feet tucked under my body in my favorite sitting position.

"She had a call from the school at the last minute. Her son's in the principal's office."

"Again?"

Shirley nodded. "That boy's a . . . well, active. Anyway, I told her not to worry about it, that I'd come alone instead of changing our regular schedule. Then I got to thinking that we might go out to grab a shake or a drink since it's just us." Her eyes narrowed. "You're not on a diet or anything, are you? You look like you've lost weight."

I didn't want to react, and if Jan had been there, I

wouldn't have, but the next minute I was crying.

Shirley scooted to the end of the couch closer to my easy chair, her arms looped over the armrest. "I didn't mean it in a bad way. You look great! Angela, what's wrong? Come on, tell me. What is it? Does this have something to do with the reason you canceled our appointment last month?"

I shook my head, then nodded. "It's nothing. I'm just not feeling well. I need to take a nap, that's all."

Shirley shook her head. "Is it Dean? One of the children? Your grandsons?"

That really made me lose it. I had five grandsons, all of whom lived out of state. I didn't get to be with them often, but I wanted to see them grow to be men. I wanted to write to them on their missions and attend their weddings.

My tears fell so fast I couldn't see Shirley anymore. I could feel her, though, kneeling by my chair, one arm around me and her other hand gripping mine. "It's okay," she murmured, as though to a small child. "It's going to be okay. Just tell me what to do, and I'll help."

"I think I need to be alone," I hiccuped, wiping my eyes impatiently. *Why, oh, why did I let her stay?*

"I'm not leaving." Shirley could be as stubborn as I was. "You don't have to tell me what's wrong if you don't want to, but I'm not leaving you here alone. So there." She lifted her chin a little, and I could see tears in her eyes.

If Jan had been there, it would have never gone this

far. Jan was a nice woman, but young and new as my visiting teacher. We hadn't yet developed the kind of friendship that Shirley and I shared.

I let myself sob for a while on Shirley's shoulder. Truthfully, it felt good to let the emotions out with someone besides my husband. My tears hurt Dean more than either of us could bear.

Finally, I composed myself enough to say, "Last month I was diagnosed with pancreatic cancer, and today I had my first chemo treatment."

"Oh, no!" Shirley gasped and held on tighter.

We both cried for a long time. As our tears slowly diminished and we regained calm, I pulled away from her and added, "You probably don't know, but pancreatic cancer is fast-growing. Very aggressive."

"Can they cut it out?" She wiped her hand over her face, blotting off the tears.

I nodded. "That's the only thing that might work."

"When are you going to have the surgery?"

This was the part I was most angry about, and for a moment my tears were held at bay by my fury. "The mass is too close to a major artery," I said tightly, "and they're afraid they'll cut it. That's why I'm having the chemo and radiation before instead of just after. I'm having chemo once every two weeks for four doses. Then I'll have radiation and more chemo for six more weeks. We won't know if any of it worked until July."

"Oh, Angela, I'm so sorry."

I could tell she really was, and for a moment my

burden slightly lifted. My anger left as quickly as it had come, leaving me dizzy and weak and tearful.

"Do they know what caused it? Why it happened?"

I shook my head. "They have no idea. Most nonhereditary cases happen after age fifty, and I'm only forty-eight." My whine grated on my own ears, but Shirley didn't seem to notice.

She looked at me solemnly. "Well, we'll get you through it, that's all. A lot of people have cancer and survive. Take my dad for instance."

I knew then that she really didn't understand. "Shirley, it's the fourth leading cause of cancer death in the United States," I spoke slowly, almost feeling removed from my body. Numb, as I'd been in the beginning. "Thirty thousand people die of it every year. Surgery is the only cure, but only five to twenty percent of people can even get the surgery. Ninety percent of people diagnosed die within the first twelve months. Fewer than five percent of patients survive five years." I'd memorized the grisly details, had taken them into my heart, and that made me glad for the numbness now. That way it didn't hurt so much.

Shirley blinked, her eyes wide and her face flushed. "Angela, you—you—I don't know what . . . you can't just—"

I cut through her stuttering, wanting no misunderstandings. Maybe even wanting to shake her with my words. "The median life expectancy after diagnosis is three months if untreated, six months with treatment."

My words had the opposite effect. She recovered her composure. "Oh, medians," she said, waving her hand to shoo the word away. "They don't mean anything."

"What?" I looked at her blankly. I'd just told her I likely had fewer than six months to live, and she acted like I'd mentioned the weather.

"Median means that half the people will die in that time. So you just make up your mind to be in the other half." She spoke as though it was an easy thing to do. "Medians don't ever mention the people who are on the far tail of the graph. Like my dad. The median for his cancer was eight months, and he didn't die for thirty years—and even then he didn't die from cancer."

I shook my head, unwilling to believe.

"Really, it's true. And they caught yours early, right?"

I nodded, though I'd learned that with the pancreas, early didn't mean curable.

"See? You're young and healthy. You've always looked after yourself, you never drank or smoked. You have support, a lot to live for. All of that will be on your side."

I didn't want to listen to her. Hope was painful at this point. "That's what the specialist told me—right before he added that I might make it a whole year."

"A pox on him!" Shirley hugged me again. "I'll come with you next time and give him a piece of my mind."

She would too—if I let her. I laughed.

Laughed. I don't know where it came from. How could anyone in my position laugh?

"That's good," Shirley said. "They say that each hour of laughing adds a day of life."

"Then I'll have to laugh an hour every day." The thought made me weary, and my smile vanished. "I just want it to go away," I said, sounding a lot like Marie when she was begging to go to the mall with her friends. "I want my life to be like it was before. I don't want to go into the future."

What I really wanted was the Lord to cure me. I wanted to know that I would see both my younger children married in the temple. But I couldn't say these last thoughts aloud, not even to Shirley.

Tears shimmered in Shirley's eyes. "Oh, Angela," she said in an oddly disappointed tone, "I know it's hard— really hard—but don't wish your life gone. Don't look behind you. You have to trust in the Lord and hear what He's trying to tell you. What He's trying to teach you."

Don't look behind you. Her words struck me hard, though I didn't know why. I wanted to cry out that she didn't understand anything. I wanted her to shut up and leave.

Don't look behind you. Where had I heard that before? I wished I could remember because suddenly it felt important—almost as though my entire future depended on knowing.

Five

Voices in the garage broke through my anger and confusion. "Looks like my kids are home." I told Shirley, wiping futilely at my cheeks. "They don't know yet."

She blinked, her mouth gaping. "They don't?"

"I haven't . . . I can't . . ."

"Go, then. I'll stall them here for a bit."

I leapt to my feet and hurried to the bathroom, still amazed that physically I wasn't feeling any different than before the chemo. I was a little light-headed, but that was from lack of food. I needed to eat.

In the downstairs bathroom, I washed my face and smeared it with lotion. Marie had left her base in the drawer, so I used a bit of that to hide the red blotches on my cheeks and around my eyes. The base made my wrinkles stand out more prominently instead of hiding them, and I wondered how I'd gotten so many. Or did I notice them more because of the fifteen pounds I'd lost?

Sighing, I pushed the thoughts aside. Really, with my diagnosis, what did a few wrinkles matter? At that I almost started crying again.

"Dear Father," I prayed, but I couldn't get the rest out. Or maybe I simply didn't know what else to say. He hadn't exactly answered my prayers lately.

Slowly, I turned from the woman in the mirror, feeling distinctly sorry for her.

Brody was in the kitchen, peering into the refrigerator, and Marie was talking to Shirley in the family room. When Marie saw me, she walked over and dropped a certificate into my hands. "I'm student of the month," she said, rotating her arms and twisting her neck slightly in a fluid I'm-so-good movement. "This is what they gave me."

"Cool," I said.

"There are coupons too." She opened a white folder with blue writing on it. "See? For a free haircut, a free donut, a free meal."

"Did they give you those 'buy one get one free' sheets?" Brody asked. "They gave those out when I was the student of the month in ninth grade."

Marie shook her head. "No."

"I never used mine anyway." He walked over to where we stood, half in the kitchen and half in the family room, his mouth full. "I gotta study for my English test with Brent, okay? He has to work later, so it's got to be now. I would have stayed after school longer if I didn't have to pick up Marie."

I knew he was asking if he could do his chores later. "Go ahead," I said. "But be home by six-thirty for dinner."

"I will." Stuffing the rest of a sandwich in his mouth, he headed for the door. Before he got there, he turned. "Oh, and I can't pick up Marie tomorrow if she has play practice. I have an after school AP study group with the teacher."

I looked at Marie. "I do have practice," she said.

"I'll pick her up," I told Brody. As he started to leave, I called after him, "Shut the garage!"

"I always do."

He did? Maybe only Marie and Dean left it open. You'd think I'd be relieved, but knowing he always closed the garage made me wonder how much else my family didn't need me for. Not exactly a comforting thought.

Shirley edged toward the door. "Well, it was nice visiting you. I'll call you tomorrow, okay? Let me know if you need anything." She looked at me significantly, but I only nodded and avoided her gaze.

Marie sat on the couch in the place Shirley had vacated, thumbing through her coupons. "I guess it's a good thing to get good grades."

This from the girl who only last week had told me she didn't think it was fair for us to require good grades.

"They wouldn't have picked you for student of the month if you hadn't been on the honor roll." I slumped into my easy chair.

She shrugged, but her smile was content. "You should have seen everyone in drama today. It was hil-ar-i-ous." She dragged out the word. "I was having a sword

38

fight with this new girl, Alison, and then this kid Josh puts out his foot and Alison trips. He tries to stop her from falling, but she lands right on him! At that exact moment, I was making a lunge, and so I fall on top of them. We were in this sort of heap, and right then the teacher turns to look at us. The other kids were laughing like crazy. We could barely explain we were all laughing so hard. My teacher blinks a couple of times and then says, 'If it was that funny, let's add it to the scene.' Can you believe that? That's what I love about drama. You can add things and be yourself. It's so fun!"

This was the real Marie, or at least the bubbly, friendly girl she'd been before puberty set in. This was the Marie who'd giggled with me when I read aloud *Cinderellis* by Gail Carson Levine and had sobbed on my shoulder when we'd read Katherine Paterson's *Bridge to Terabithia*. She was the one who had always eagerly curled up next to me on the couch to watch the chick flick videos I brought home.

Marie continued to talk—about her classes, her friends, what she had due the next day for homework. I knew I should get up and think about making dinner, but I was too emotionally drained to consider climbing out of my chair.

"I'd better get to my math." Marie finally arose, leaving her purse and a few stray papers on the couch. She was always leaving things behind her.

"Marie," I said.

"What?"

"Never mind." I didn't want to destroy the moment. "Congratulations on being student of the month."

I must have fallen asleep in the chair, because when I awoke, the light outside the window had faded. The house was utterly quiet. Then I heard a page turn.

"Mom? Are you awake?"

I craned my neck and saw Marie at the kitchen table, studiously working on her advanced algebra assignment.

"Do you need help?" My mouth was dry, and I wished for a drink of water.

Marie came over and stood in front of me, her eyes wary.

She's going to ask if she can go somewhere even though Dean grounded her, somewhere she knows I won't like, I thought. *Oh, please, not now.* A wave of nausea shuddered through me, and I wondered if I'd have time to make it to the bathroom. I clenched my stomach muscles, and the urge slowly receded.

"Is something wrong?" Marie sat on the edge of the couch close to my chair. "Why are you sleeping?" Her eyes narrowed. "You're not pregnant, are you?"

I tried to laugh, but it came out sounding more like a strangled snort. "No, I am definitely not pregnant." What's more, the chemo would make sure I never would be again. For some reason, that deeply saddened me. Though I never planned to have another child, losing part of what made me a woman wasn't easy.

"Good. Becki's mother told her today that they're having another baby. Can you believe it?"

"Well, Becki is the oldest, and her parents don't have that many kids."

"Yeah, but if it's a girl, Becki's going to have to share her room with one of her sisters."

"I shared a room my whole life growing up."

Marie rolled her eyes. "I know. And you used to walk to school, and you had no computer or cell phones or iPods. I'm glad I wasn't born back then." Tossing her head, she stood and returned to her math.

I arose and walked slowly to the phone to call Dean.

He picked up immediately. "Are you all right?" he asked, his tone anxious.

"Yes, but could you bring home something for dinner?"

"No problem. Is someone there with you?"

"Marie." My daughter looked up as I said her name, but her eyes were clouded with concentration. I doubted she even heard me ask Dean to bring food. If she had, she might become suspicious.

"Good. Get some rest, then. See you in a bit."

I hung up the phone, a strange heaviness spreading over my body. "Marie," I said. "I'm going upstairs to my room. Tell your dad, okay?"

The staircase had never looked so long, but gripping the railing, I somehow made it up to my room. Marie didn't notice my tedious progress.

The next thing I knew, Dean was waking me, a plate of Chinese takeout in his hand. "Hi, sleepyhead. How do you feel?"

"Fine, great. Well, a little tired." I smiled. "I'm glad we went to the planetarium yesterday and not today." I sat up as he put a pillow behind my back. I tried to eat for him, and after a few bites, the food made my stomach feel better.

"Want some ice cream?" he asked. "I bought your favorite."

"Caramel swirl?"

"Of course."

"All right. Where are the kids?"

"Downstairs. I got a video."

Tenderness swelled in my heart at his thoughtful attention to detail, until he spoiled it by adding, "We need to tell them."

"Not yet."

"When?"

"I don't know."

"I could do it."

"No." I shoved my still-heaping plate at him. "I can't eat any more."

His smile this time was fake, but his voice was gentle. "I'll get your ice cream."

If I still had the plate, I would have thrown it at his retreating back. Didn't he understand that I didn't want him to be nice? I didn't want him to have any kind of faith. I wanted him to be as angry and upset and betrayed as I felt.

Then as suddenly as my anger flared, it vanished, leaving me weak and weepy.

My eyes were suddenly so heavy, as though weights had been placed on the lids. I let them shut, willing sleep to take me. At least sleeping, I didn't have to confront the moment. I didn't have to wonder about the future.

Sometime later I awoke. The room was dark and still. Dean wasn't in bed next to me, but I could see the lump of his head as he knelt beside the bed praying. He was there a long time, and I began to breathe lightly and shallowly for fear of disturbing him. At the same time I felt bitter. What good would praying do? Once I wouldn't have dared question the power of prayer, but now my life hung in the balance. Everything was different.

Dean believed. Or was he simply going through the motions as I had begun doing?

I wished I could pray with faith. Maybe then I could understand what the Lord was doing to me.

Six

"Honey, it's time." Dean's voice came to me from far away.

I opened my eyes and nodded, seeing that morning had already arrived.

"How are you?"

I wish he'd stop asking me that. "Fine."

"You can stay here. I'll read scriptures with the kids."

"No, I want to say good-bye." The day wouldn't be the same if I couldn't hug them as I always did before they left for school.

I could barely get out of bed, and each step required my full focus. They'd warned me this might happen after a chemo treatment, but I had felt so good yesterday, aside from being tired last night, that this overwhelming weakness and exhaustion came as a shock.

I let Dean help me down the stairs to the family room where Brody was waiting with his scriptures. Marie was in the bathroom but emerged as we passed and followed us to the couch. Neither child noticed I was leaning on Dean. Why were my legs so heavy?

Dean opened the window blinds so we had more light to read by. I was surprised to see rain outside, the moisture dripping silently down the window and the railings of our redwood deck. Like tears that dripped soundlessly down a human face.

I dozed on and off through scripture study, awaking only when Dean nudged me and pointed to the scripture I was supposed to read. After prayer, Brody left for the high school while Marie made her last dash to the bathroom to fix her hair for what was probably the tenth time that morning and to make sure all her blemishes were adequately covered with makeup.

"Hurry up, Marie!" Frustration crept into Dean's voice. He always dropped her off at the junior high on his way to work but hated waiting while she primped. "We need to go."

Marie emerged from the bathroom. "Mom," she said, scooping up several books and a folder, "could you take me to use one of those coupons I got for student of the month when you pick me up?"

Dean answered for me. "She's not picking you up today. You can walk. Your mother's not feeling well."

"But it's all rainy and cold." Marie pointed to the gray world beyond the window. "I don't want to walk home in that. I don't have a coat."

"What about that jacket I bought you?" I asked, rallying my strength.

"I can't find it."

"Again?" That explained why she was wearing only

a snug, thin shirt with tiny capped sleeves. All the girls wore these, but on cold days most put sweaters or jackets on top.

Marie shrugged, avoiding my gaze, and I knew she must have looked for the jacket without success.

"You can wear mine." I had a new one that would look great on her.

She pursed her lips. "Uh—no. I'd rather freeze."

Kindness incarnate was not my daughter.

Marie saw my face and added quickly. "I mean thanks, but I'll be fine, really. Your jacket's nice, but it's not my style." That meant no one wore jackets like mine in the ninth grade. I wasn't offended. Who wanted to look like a ninth-grader?

"I'm sure I'll be able to pick her up," I told Dean. "I was just a little tired when I woke up. I'm fine now."

Dean studied me doubtfully, but he didn't challenge my words, as I knew he wouldn't. "Let's go," he said at last to Marie. He leaned down and planted a fleeting kiss on my mouth, and I caught the familiar scent of his aftershave. Even as little as five weeks ago, I would have put my arms around his neck and insisted on a real kiss, but I felt too self-conscious now, as though the cancer inside had irreparably changed who I had been before, turning me from a whole and valid person into something . . . well, something less.

Marie started for the door, then gasped. "I forgot my gym clothes!" Throwing her armload to the couch, she raced upstairs to her room.

Dean sighed. "That girl is going to be the death of me." Then, as if realizing what he'd said, his face crumpled. I sat on the couch looking up at him, and he stood staring down at me. There was so much to say, but not enough words in any language we knew. I looked away first.

Marie ran into the family room and scooped up her books and folder. Dean bent down to kiss me again. "Call me if you need me," he whispered in my ear. "I'll try to be home early."

"Bye, Mom!" Marie tossed over her shoulder as she hurried out the door.

All at once I was alone. This was the time of the day that I usually lingered over breakfast and the newspaper. Often I'd written down ideas for my restaurant. I'd wanted an open-fire grill where the cook would baste whole chickens right behind the counter in plain view of the customer. I'd tasted such savory chicken in Boston once and had asked for the recipe from the Portuguese cook, who'd been flattered enough to give it to me. In my restaurant I'd also planned to offer homemade potato chips, salad, and European pastries that would please the eyes as much as the palate. There would be a section of the restaurant to eat in if you were in the mood to socialize, but takeout would be the norm. Though we lived in Lindon, I had my eye on a place in downtown Pleasant Grove that I thought would be the perfect location. I wouldn't worry about having a variety but would focus on simple, solid, tasty food that would keep people coming back at least once a week. In the summer, maybe people would eat in the park down the street, or I could set a table or two out on the sidewalk.

Today I didn't want to think about the restaurant. I fixed myself dry toast and lay down on the couch. The scriptures Marie had left on the cushion were digging into the back of my shoulders, but I was too tired to care. Maybe if I took a nap, I'd get my strength back.

Sleep wouldn't come. I felt helpless, lying there with heavy limbs and no chance of escape. So this was chemotherapy. Even now, the drugs—poisons, really—were in my veins, coursing through my entire body. I hoped it found the cancer before it destroyed something more vital.

Shivering, I made a great effort to turn over. How could something that was always so easy suddenly become so difficult?

My gaze landed on Marie's scriptures. Without volition, my eyes took in the words of Mosiah 27:11.

Another angel. If I'd had enough energy, I would have thrown the book across the room, hopefully breaking something in the process. Instead, I squeezed my eyes shut.

I walked through the fields, enjoying the lush landscape around me despite the heat beating down overhead and the humidity that made my skin shine. The harvest would be good this year, and after all the work and prayers we'd put into the fields, we deserved the bounty. The Lord had blessed us greatly.

Again I carried a water jar, presumably for those in the fields. But it was empty, and my tunic and thin mantel were drenched as though I had spilled some of the water— perhaps not so accidentally, given the heat.

I was leaving the fields when I saw them. Four youth in bright clothing—reds and even purple were prominent, and I knew from my Book of Mormon studies that I was in the presence of royalty.

They didn't speak like royalty. They were cursing and laughing coarsely about some wrong they had done.

I shuddered, realizing I might not be safe if I met these boys on this hard-packed dirt road alone. I searched for a place to hide.

The bright cloud appeared suddenly, but for me not unexpectedly.

An angel spoke from the cloud, his voice thunderous. The ground shook with the sound, and I fell to the ground. The boys also fell, their faces frozen in shock. I couldn't decipher the angel's words, but I knew they were glorious.

"Look at me," I whispered. "Heal me."

The angel spoke again, and one of the youths stood clumsily, after several failed attempts. I knew he was Alma the Younger being chastised for persecuting the Church.

I listened harder. Maybe there was a message for me. My heart yearned to understand.

The angel continued, and this time I understood. "Behold, the Lord hath heard the prayers of his people, and also the prayers of his servant, Alma, who is thy father; for he has prayed with much faith concerning thee that thou mightest be brought to the knowledge of the truth; therefore, for this purpose have I come to convince thee of the power and authority of God, that the prayers of his servants might be answered according to their faith."

Faith. I'd had faith all my life, or so I thought, but now it was gone. All gone.

Yet because of prayer, Alma and the sons of Mosiah had become powerful men of God. They would save thousands of souls.

I opened my eyes. *At least Alma the Elder had a problem child too*, I thought.

This witness of the power of prayer reminded me of Dean on his knees last night. There had been a time when we would have prayed together, but I couldn't pray with him anymore. I'd gone to bed early or later— anything to avoid that intimacy. I didn't want to hear him praying for me. It was one thing if my prayers went unanswered, but I couldn't bear to hear Dean pleading in vain.

Tears wet my face. There were no sobs or heaving of shoulders that usually mark a bout of crying. Rather, the tears silently angled sideways down my face as I lay there, like the rain I'd witnessed earlier. Like blood seeping from a wound.

I'd fallen to my lowest low ever, and what frightened me more was that I knew this was only the beginning—either the beginning of my escape from death or the beginning of that death. Unfortunately, the statistics didn't hold out much hope for escape.

There was no sound but the drizzling rain as I bled tears and thought about my lost life. About Alma the Elder praying for his son.

I didn't want my children to lose their mother. Could I pray at least for them?

I must have slept, but I awoke sometime later with my stomach growling. I gathered enough strength to roll over and managed to get to my feet. Slowly, I walked to the kitchen to get myself some bread and maybe a glass of milk. The phone rang on my return trip to the couch.

I made a detour to pick it up. "Hello?"

"It's me," Dean said.

"Hi, honey."

"How are you?"

I sank to a kitchen chair, bracing myself on the table. "I'm about to have lunch."

"You need help?"

"No, I'm fine. I'm tired, but there's not a lot of pain or anything." *Yet*, I added to myself.

"Good. I'm showing a few houses to a couple right now, but I could send someone over with lunch. Or I could come after I finish."

"No, stay. I have food here. After I eat, I'll go back to sleep."

"Okay, I love you."

"I love you too."

We hung up, and I methodically ate two pieces of bread and drank my glass of milk. No sooner had I swallowed the last bit than the nausea returned in force.

I heaved, clapping my hand over my mouth, barely making it to the bathroom to throw up. Again and again I heaved, and still heaved long after there was nothing left to come. I sat braced against the wall until I was able to make my way unsteadily back to the couch. I took the bread sack with me and, after lying down, ate a half a piece, much more slowly than before. My limbs were heavier now, and my eyes drooped. The nausea was worse than the growling of my empty stomach, so I decided to rest and try eating later.

The answering machine woke me. "Angela? It's me, Shirley. Are you all right? Please give me a call. I'm at home if you need anything."

I couldn't get up. A short time later the doorbell rang, but I didn't even try to leave the couch. I reread the scriptures in Mosiah instead. I felt a little like Alma the Younger after he'd fallen. My limbs refused to obey me, and my whole body was beginning to ache. Maybe if I slept a little more.

"Mom," Marie's voice came from far away. "Where are you? I thought you were going to pick me up. It's pouring rain out there. I'm freezing, and my books will get all wet. Mom? Did you forget about me? Mom?" The answering machine clicked off.

I blinked. How had the time flown so quickly? I had to get Marie! I turned, managing to roll off the couch again, but instead of rising I fell to the floor, and that was where I stayed. Hurt exploded through my senses, more an all-encompassing unwellness than any specific pain.

The journey to the door seemed like miles, and I didn't even know where I'd left my car keys. I began crawling to the phone to call Dean, but a strong bout of nausea stopped my halting progress. I sobbed at my helplessness.

Marie would have to walk—alone, in the rain, and in the premature dark that was already falling outside.

Please watch over my daughter, I prayed.

How easy it was to pray for someone else, especially when it was such a simple thing. Marie didn't need an angel or anything. She would be drenched, feel angry, and maybe catch a cold, but she would survive.

A short time later, I heard the garage door opening. I was still on the floor but pulled myself onto the couch seconds before the door opened.

"Mom!" Marie burst into the house. She wasn't wet or shivering. "You're here? How come you didn't pick up the phone?"

I turned to her weakly. "I got sick. I threw up."

Marie frowned. "I guess it's a good thing Sister Jefferson showed up."

It was then I saw Shirley behind my daughter. She was still outside in the garage, which was why I hadn't noticed her before, but she came inside now, smiling tentatively. "I just happened by the school," she explained, "and I knew you weren't feeling that great yesterday, so I thought I'd give Marie a ride."

Shirley had no reason to be near the junior high. The school was out of the way, and her last child was already in high school.

"Thanks," I said.

"I'm sorry you're sick, Mom, but at least that explains why you went to sleep so early last night." Marie started across the room. "I'd better get my math done before Mutual. We're having it early tonight. First I want to change."

Early? I didn't even have dinner ready—and wouldn't by the looks of things.

As Marie left to go upstairs to her room, Shirley came over to the couch. "I tried to call earlier," she said.

"I couldn't get to the phone. I've been sick."

"I thought as much. My father would stay in bed for two days after his"—she glanced behind her at the open railing to the second floor, but Marie was nowhere to be seen—"chemo treatments. Look, I'm bringing dinner, and nothing you can say will stop me. I made enough casserole for half the block."

"You don't have to do that. Dean'll be home soon."

"He should be home now." Her voice was clipped. "And if he won't be, I will. Angela, you can't do this alone."

"I don't want to do it at all!" My chest started heaving, and I knew I was going to either throw up or cry. I hated Shirley at that moment. I hated everyone. I wanted to die and get it over with. What was the use of even trying? I was going to die anyway.

Shirley didn't speak. She simply sat down and watched me with huge, watery eyes.

Marie appeared in the adjoining kitchen moments

later, her math book under her arm. "Hey, what's up with you two, anyway? You act like you're at a funeral or something." She chuckled at her own wit, and my heart twisted again. Though she didn't mean anything by it, she'd regret that remark someday.

Memories flooded over me.

"Mom," I'd said one day a couple of months before her death, "you have to be more careful." She'd taken too many pain pills, not because she'd wanted to, but because she couldn't remember how many she'd taken, and she'd still been sleeping when I came home from school. The drug had made her heartbeat irregular, and the doctor had warned her that the effects could be potentially deadly.

Mom had laughed. "Don't worry, honey. I'm not going anywhere."

"Good." I gave her my best deadpan. "Because I really don't have time to attend a funeral, what with my great debut and all." We'd both laughed ourselves silly.

Later, after the accidental overdose that took her life, there was nothing funny about it.

"Well," Shirley stood. "I'm going to zip home and see if my rolls are ready for baking. I'll be back in about twenty minutes."

That she'd left rolls rising verified my suspicions; she'd gone to the school just for Marie.

In a way, I supposed my daughter had a sort of angel in Shirley. How odd that the Lord would send Marie an angel when I was the one who needed one. But I would take whatever we could get; I wanted the best for my daughter.

After Shirley left, I said to Marie, "Shut the garage for me, okay?"

"Okay, just a minute." She finished the problem she was working on before going to the door. "Uh, Mom," she said, "Dad's out there. He's talking to Sister Jefferson. Oh, here he comes." Marie went back to her homework.

Dean came in, leaving the garage door open. I decided it didn't matter. I'd close it before I went up to bed—provided I could get to my feet by then.

Dean knelt by the couch where I lay sprawled, my head on top of Marie's scriptures. He eased them out from under me. "Why didn't you tell me?" he asked, his voice gruff.

Because I didn't want you to look at me like that.

There were looks that women craved from the men they loved—admiration, awe, trust, and especially that certain something between husband and wife that signaled intimacy. But not pity. That was one look a woman never needed to see from the man she loved.

"I was fine," I said, my eyes filling with tears.

He hugged me. "No," he whispered. "You're not fine, but we're going to make you that way."

Good luck, I thought. He was going to need a lot of help.

Twenty minutes later, Shirley arrived with dinner.

Seven

My sickness and exhaustion lasted only one more day. By Friday, I was up and about, feeling relatively normal, as though there was nothing really wrong with me at all and the horror of the past days something I'd imagined. I still had an occasional pain in my abdomen and experienced periodic nausea, but that was nothing new.

Dean urged me to tell the children, but I begged for more time. I wanted first to know what direction I was headed before I ruined their lives. I think deep down I wanted to offer them the hope that I couldn't find for myself.

The next two weeks rolled by smoothly. I no longer thought about my restaurant or made up lists of things I would need to buy before I could open. I didn't clean house more than absolutely necessary, and I didn't do anything in my calling as ward music chairman. Instead, I focused on my family. I bought cards and presents for all my grandsons and sent them off. I spent hours quizzing Brody for his AP exam, and his gratitude made me feel needed and loved. I took Marie wherever she and her friends wanted to go, volunteering to supervise every activity. I tried not to feel hurt when she didn't thank me or acknowledge my presence.

"That child thinks of nothing but herself," Dean said to me one day. Once I would have commiserated with him, but now I was happy Marie could still be selfish. Maybe selfish was the definition of fourteen. What fourteen-year-old girl ever looked for sadness on her mother's face? What fourteen-year-old ever did her chores as well as her parents would like? What fourteen-year-old didn't brag about her day and not ask anyone else what kind of day they'd had? What fourteen-year-old noticed when her mother lost weight or cried in the night?

I had managed to give birth to one daughter who hadn't been a typical teen—Sharon. She had always been sensitive to my needs. As a young woman, she'd often called me from her babysitting jobs to ask how I was doing. Dean once told me that he always knew if Sharon was on the phone because he heard me say, "I love you too" instead of "I love you." Sharon had always seemed to be as happy spending time with me as with her friends, and I missed her living at home. She had married last year, at barely twenty, earlier than any of the others. I'd wanted to object, but how could I when I'd married Dean at that exact same age? Sharon's husband was twenty-two, a returned missionary whose gray eyes lit up every time he looked at her. I felt they would make it, as Dean and I had.

If Sharon had been living at home, I wouldn't have been able to fool her. Despite her busy schedule in college, she still called home three times a week, and so far I'd managed to direct our conversations away from me. She was happy, in love, and expecting her first baby. I didn't want to take any of that joy away from her.

My older three boys hadn't called, and my other daughter had called only once since the diagnosis. There wasn't any need for covering up there. They were all content in their lives, and I was determined to leave it that way for as long as possible.

"Are you ready?" Dean asked.

I looked at Dean, who had been tidying the kitchen. Today I had to go in for more chemotherapy. Two weeks had passed, and my body was supposed to be recovered enough for another dose. Of course we hoped cancer cells wouldn't be growing at their previous rapid rate, but it would be months before we knew if the plan had worked enough for me to get the surgery.

"I'm ready," I said, forcing my voice to be light.

The drive to the hospital went faster than expected. Though I'd been through it once before, I was feeling nervous when we entered, but the nurses again quickly put me at ease. They offered me pillows and magazines before taking a blood sample through my port. If my white blood cell count was too low, they wouldn't be able to give the chemo drugs to me. I passed with flying colors.

They also offered me water, as I was supposed to

be well-hydrated the four hours before receiving one of the drugs, but I'd already had enough liquids to make me visit the bathroom twice in the last hour. That drug alone took nearly two hours to administer.

After an hour, Dean became restless, so I sent him to the cafeteria to buy an early lunch. "Do you want anything?" he asked.

"Maybe a roll," I said. Bread was my staple nowadays. "White, not wheat." For whatever reason, I couldn't eat wheat bread without throwing up.

"I'll see if they have a banana too." He'd been making sandwiches out of them for me, sometimes with a bit of peanut butter, as bananas were the only fruit I seemed to tolerate well these days. I was sick of both bananas and bread, but I always made an effort to eat the sandwiches when he brought them, knowing it was one of the few things he felt he could do to help me.

The nurses had changed me to the next drug when a lady with graying hair settled in the empty chair next to mine in preparation for her treatment. I was curious about her, but Dean was the one who usually initiated personal questions to the other patients.

I'd already met Willy across from me, an old man with liver cancer, and the middle-aged man next to him called Joe, who hadn't volunteered his diagnosis. Beyond Joe was a little boy named Eric who had leukemia and was there with both his parents. The mother's eyes were red, and she held her little boy's hand so tightly, he kept complaining. His father sat with his arms folded across his chest, looking like someone had hit him in the stomach. Sandy, a sober, black-haired woman barely in her thirties, sat on my other side. She had breast cancer.

The new woman smiled at me. "This is my last time here." Her face folded into wrinkles as she smiled, but her brown eyes were bright and alive.

I hoped that meant she'd been cured and not that they were giving up.

"You mean it's still gone?" called the old man opposite us.

"That's right, Willy. I'm cured." She shrugged. "Well, you know how that goes. Last week my doctor told me it could come back any minute." She deepened her voice to mimic him. "That's the kind of cancer it is, Mrs. Jones."

"Old Dr. Snell," Willy said with a snort. "He don't have a compassionate bone in his body, I don't think."

"Nonsense," the woman said. "He just doesn't like to lead us on, that's all. And I don't mind. I don't intend to come back here ever." There was a finality to her words, as though she would rather go to the next life than endure chemotherapy again.

"Like you said, that's what kind of cancer it is," Willy said. "There's only so much surgery they can do."

"What kind of cancer was it?" I asked.

She looked at me and smiled. "Pancreatic."

"Really? Me too." I know it's stupid, but I felt an immediate kinship with this woman. She was the first one I'd met with my cancer, and to hear her talk, she was cured! That would put her in the ten percent who survived more than a year. That meant she now had a fifty percent chance of surviving beyond five years. Looking at her gave me hope.

"Hi, I'm Betty Jones. Are you new? I mean, newly diagnosed?"

I nodded. "Sort of. This is my second time here."

"Then you've had the surgery?"

"No. The growth is too close to an artery. They're trying to shrink it."

Betty looked concerned. "Who's your doctor?"

"Dr. Snell."

She relaxed. "He's the best. You're in good hands."

"I haven't met any others," I said.

"You mean with our kind of cancer. There were some I met here." A shadow passed over Betty's face. "Well, they put up a good fight. I'm sure there's more we haven't met."

I wasn't so sure—unless they were newly diagnosed like I was.

Betty kept up a steady stream of conversation. She talked about her two children and her six grandchildren. She mentioned her husband, who'd died of a heart attack two years earlier.

"I'm sorry," I said, wondering how I could have faced this without Dean.

Betty shrugged. "It's life. There's no use looking behind us. We just go forward and find happiness where we can. The good Lord knows what He's doing." With a wave of her hand, she took in all the chairs and the poles that loomed over us—each supporting a bag of clear liquid poison that was supposed to cure us. "There's a reason for this, even if we don't know what that is right now. Like I said, no use looking behind us."

No use looking behind us. Where had I heard that before?

Then I remembered Shirley. I'd become angry at her because I knew she couldn't possibly understand, but I couldn't say the same about Betty. She'd gone through all of this with only her married children—a son in St. George and a daughter in Houston—for support.

No use looking behind.

I felt as though Betty was telling me some secret that I couldn't understand. I heard the words, but my mind simply didn't stretch wide enough to let in the meaning.

"I'm leaving this weekend to visit my daughter and grandchildren in Houston," Betty continued. "I'm going to stay as long as I'm wanted."

Betty was a delightful woman, and I didn't think her daughter would ever want to send her away. But you never could tell how a child would react—even a grown one.

Don't look behind you. Why did that still stick in my mind? Where else had I heard it before?

Then I knew.

With an anticipation I hadn't felt in six weeks, I reached for my pocket PC that I'd carried in my purse since Dean had given it to me for Christmas to track the

family schedules. Brody had helped me put the scriptures on the device, but I had rarely used them, always
preferring the feel of a book in my hands. Now I was
grateful to have them with me.

Betty Jones must have seen something in my face;
she fell silent and pulled out a colorful, half-finished
afghan from the bag on her lap.

I clicked to Genesis thirteen and began reading.

Eight

Wind whipped sand into my eyes, and I was grateful for the wool cloth draped over my mouth. The hot sun beat down from above, and underneath my plain tunic and head covering, I was drenched in sweat. Up ahead I heard the call to stop.

"Sodom lies ahead," a woman next to me said, pointing down the gentle slope we'd been following. "Many people dwell there."

In the distance I could barely make out a walled settlement, full of homes made of mud bricks, the roofs covered in palm fronds. Most of the structures were only one story, but a few rose as high as two.

"There's a marketplace," said the woman with admiration. "We will trade well. Master Lot is wise to bring us to this place."

I followed the woman and helped her pass food to the men and then to a large group of wide-eyed children. She told them we were almost at our destination.

I couldn't believe they were going to Sodom. Didn't they understand how dangerous it was? Surely the city's *reputation preceded it. I opened my mouth to speak but couldn't. Apparently, there was a limit to my participation.*

After the short break the people and cattle began moving again. We were off the slope now, and Sodom's innards were hidden from sight. The walk was interminable, but the men, women, and children bore it with ease and few complaints. I seemed to be the only one having difficulty.

At last we stopped, and this time I helped the women unload the donkeys and pitch the heavy, black, goat-haired tents. I froze when Lot directed the people to face his tent in the direction of Sodom. Tears trickled from my eyes, already stinging from the desert sand. Around me, Lot's people cheered.

"I am pleased that my husband chose to go with Master Lot instead of following Master Abraham," the woman of earlier said. "Else we would not have been so close to a city as prosperous as this one."

Hindsight would reveal that Lot had not made a wise decision. No student of the Bible was ever surprised when God later destroyed the sinful city with brimstone and fire.

Abraham, I knew, would settle in Hebron, where he would build an altar and offer sacrifice unto the Lord. Years from now, he would even save Lot from captivity and refuse reward from the king of Sodom, not willing to associate with such wickedness. Later still, he would be given a promised child by his beloved Sarah.

I was certainly in the wrong place. Here was Lot, his family, and herdsmen facing, yearning, longing for a city of known evil.

What a fool, *I thought scornfully.* Doesn't he know that it's only a matter of time before his children are drawn to the children of Sodom? Only a few years until they become so entrenched that nothing will be able to save them?

Not even an angel.

Helplessness engulfed me. Why was I here? Surely I was still back at the hospital receiving my treatment, reading the story that had come to life before me. I willed myself to wake. I knew exactly what came next, and I didn't want to be there for it.

Sands around me shifted until I was standing in what appeared to be a mud brick house with a low ceiling. Lot was talking to several men, who made no show of hiding their mockery.

"Up," Lot said, "get you out of this place; for the Lord will destroy this city."

The men refused. Lot left them, and I followed, listening to the mocking laughter filling the house and trailing after us. We pursued a narrow alleyway for some time until he halted at another mud brick house. A woman met him at the door. "Good husband, give me thy tidings."

Lot shook his head, his shoulders bowed, and she seemed to crumple in on herself. I bit my lower lip as I watched her tears fall.

I knew we were in Sodom then and that Abraham had already asked the Lord to save the city for the sake of the righteous. Surely, he'd pleaded, there were at least fifty righteous people in the city. Yet the Lord could not find fifty righteous people, so Abraham's plea dwindled to forty-five, forty, thirty, twenty, and then at last ten. Finally only his nephew Lot and his family were to be spared.

But Lot's sons-in-law mocked the word of the Lord and their father and would not be saved. Lot put his arms around his wife and mourned with her.

I sat on a stool nearby and watched the heartbreak around me. I knew Lot now regretted coming to Sodom. He finally understood the danger he had placed his family in, and there was no heart left in the man to go on. I knew exactly how he felt. It wasn't easy knowing that everything—or almost everything—was lost.

I stumbled out to their small courtyard and fell to my knees. "Why, Father? I don't understand." For long moments I prayed, seeking an answer. There had to be some connection between all these experiences I was having and my own life. But what? Darkness fell, and I slept.

The sun had not yet completely risen again when I heard a commotion in the small house. I went toward the sounds.

Two angels in the form of men were in the main room with Lot and his wife. "Arise," one said to Lot, "take thy wife, and thy two daughters, which are here; lest thou be consumed in the iniquity of the city."

Lot lingered still, and the angels took hold upon him and his wife and two daughters, bringing them out of the city. Laden on donkeys were all their worldly possessions. Tears made paths down our cheeks. Lot's wife had the look of a woman who had lost all that she held most dear.

The heat bore down on my covered head. For miles around us stretched sand. Even the surrounding mountains were nothing more than sand and dirt. Several hardy acacia trees appeared along the way, but even these were scraggly and twisted.

Someone was sobbing, and I didn't want to lift my head to see who it was. "This is too hard," I whispered. "Why am I here?"

The angels stopped walking and faced Lot. "Escape for thy life; look not behind thee, neither to stay thou in all the plain; escape to the mountain, lest thou be consumed."

Look not behind thee.

I knew he wasn't only talking to Lot and his family, but to me. Me. Angela Thornberry.

Strangely, as soon as the request was made and the angels were gone on their way, I had the most forceful desire to look behind me. Why not take just a peek? What would it hurt? Surely the view of fire and brimstone falling from the sky would be an incredible show of power! I wanted to see it. I would never have such an opportunity again.

Yet the angel said not to look back.

When I'd first heard this story in primary, I thought anyone would have been stupid to not follow the advice of an angel. Yet here I was, tempted. I was dying anyway—what would it hurt?

That was when it happened. Lot's wife gave an agonized cry and looked back. Then she was gone, and in her place stood a pillar of salt.

I fell to my knees, hearing the keening of her family but

unable to focus on their faces. A pillar of salt. Surely curios-
ity or worry for your children wouldn't condemn a person to
be licked up by a couple of donkeys!

My breath came hard. If I had looked, then what?

"What does it mean?" I begged, staring up into the roil-
ing, angry, black clouds that filled the entire sky. I knew
what it meant for Lot's wife. She had looked back and had
paid the price—a horrible price! But what did it have to
do with me?

I closed my eyes, which were stinging from the soot that
hung on the air in heavy dark clouds. I could hear the others
moving on. I didn't want to be here alone.

I jumped to my feet, but the scene before me had
changed. I was back outside Sodom years earlier with Lot
and his people as they pitched their tents. Sweat trickled
down my covered scalp and down the middle of my back.

It's all connected, *I thought, watching Lot and his*
wife standing by their tent and looking toward Sodom. I
could see they were interested in its glittery attractiveness
and glory even though the "men of Sodom were wicked and
sinners before the Lord."

This was where it began, the first step toward the day
when Lot's wife looked back. So what did that mean for me?
As I pondered, I felt a communication spirit to spirit as was
supposed to happen when you feast on the scriptures.

In that crystal moment, I understood that Lot's wife
hadn't simply looked back. She hadn't wanted to leave at
all. Her heart had yearned to stay with those of her family
left behind. She hadn't believed or wanted to hear what the

angel told her about the coming destruction. Or perhaps she had rationalized the wickedness around her, having grown accustomed to the face of evil. She'd wanted to stay in Sodom and tend her home and grandchildren.

So did I. I wanted my life to be as it was before my diagnosis. I yearned to return to the path I'd traveled and wished to escape the future I'd been given. I wanted to be there for my family regardless of what the Lord wanted. In a very real way, I had been trying to remain in my own Sodom. No, my life hadn't been full of evil, but I was stuck without progression as Lot and his family had been. My unwillingness to go forward and accept the Lord's will was as clearly an act of looking back as what Lot's wife had done. If not for the two angels in my life, first Shirley and now Betty Jones, who had both urged me to stop looking back and make the best of what I had left, I might have experienced the same spiritual punishment meted out to Lot's wife.

I gazed around me again, my heart lifting with this clear understanding. It had started here in this very spot in this exact moment in time. Overhead, the sky, now a deep and incredible blue, reached from horizon to horizon, achingly beautiful.

To avoid looking back, I needed to learn from Lot's example. I needed to pitch my tent not toward Sodom, which represented my old life and understanding, but toward the Lord. I needed to hear His words and understand what this experience was supposed to teach me. Now was the time to prove I would listen and not trade my future for a block of salt.

I looked up from the words, smiling. I'd already been given so much, including these precious glimpses of scriptures that had echoed happenings in my own life: Dean defending me as the angel defended Nephi, Dean praying for me as Alma prayed for his son, Shirley and Betty urging me not to look back. I didn't completely understand the vision of Sarah and her miracle baby yet, but even Isaac's birth had been to my benefit, for I was of the lineage of Ephraim, who was Sarah's great-great-grandson. Her miracle was partly my own.

I didn't know exactly how I would accomplish the task, but I vowed I would not look behind me again. Maybe if I didn't, I could find some way to step forward.

Nine

Dean returned, but I was so filled with my discovery and the hope it gave to the barren landscape of my heart that I could barely speak. I sat clutching my pocket PC and trying to explain, glad the woman on my right had finished her treatment and was gone, allowing us more privacy.

"I set my tent toward Sodom," I told Dean in a whisper. "But you probably knew that all along. I'm so sorry, honey."

His blue eyes darkened as he squinted at me in concern. "It's okay, Angela." He moved closer. "There's no tent, but I'm here. Don't worry."

"It's not a real tent." I tried not to be annoyed, which I suspected would destroy the feelings of peace in my heart. "It's a symbol to help me not look behind."

I glanced at Betty, hoping for backup or at least for her to repeat her words about the Lord knowing what He was doing, but she was dozing now, her afghan lying across her thin chest, the crochet needle still in her hand. The bright colors made a stark contrast to her pale face and gray hair.

Tears welled in Dean's eyes as he ran his hand firmly up and down my arm. "It's the drugs, honey. Remember what the doctor said? You might be confused, but it will pass in a while. Look, do you want me to get the nurse? Your medication seems to be almost finished. I'll take you home. I have a roll and a banana for you. You can eat them in the car."

His eyes held tenderness, love, and more than a trace of terror. I could tell he was only able to bear this situation because of his love for me. Dear Dean. My dearest, lovely husband. My angel. How did I get so lucky?

"I'm not confused. I've been reading about Lot and Sodom." I handed him my pocket PC. "You can read it for yourself."

He glanced down at the words, but I could tell he was still worried and not really paying attention. Maybe it didn't mean the same thing to him. Maybe facing death was something everyone had to do in their own way.

I was relieved when the nurse came to take the needle from my port, freeing me from the chair. Dean helped me stand and put his arm around me as we started for the door.

"Wait," I said. Fumbling in my purse, I found the business cards Sharon had printed up as part of my Christmas gift. "It's for when you run into old friends," she'd explained. "Or when you meet new ones you want to keep in touch with." In the space Sharon had left for a short note, I wrote

Good luck in Houston. If you have time to write, I'd love to hear how you're doing.
Angela Thornberry

Dean kept his arm around me as we walked to the car. We drove in silence to the house.

We knew what to expect this time. I'd feel fairly well for the rest of the day, if a little tired, but the following two days, I'd be lucky to climb from my bed. I had two dinners waiting in the refrigerator that only required heating up.

Two treatments left, I thought. Of course, that was deceptive, since those would be followed by daily radiation, additional chemo on the weekend, and hopefully the surgery and more chemo. But at least I was moving forward.

Hours later the children came home, bubbling with enthusiasm and energy. "You should have seen me in volleyball today, Mom!" Marie burst out the moment she arrived home. "We played in PE. Alison knows all sorts of plays since she's on a team, and I'm really good. I could get it over the net every time." She laughed. "You should have seen Becki, though. She was hilarious. She couldn't hit it at all. It kept rolling up her arms and hitting her in the face. But I'm a natural. Alison said I should play on a team."

That was my daughter, full of confidence. Sometimes I wonder where she got her ego, since neither Dean nor I so blatantly flaunted our talents.

"Yeah, yeah, you're the best. We've heard it before." Brody smiled as he said the words, taking out much of the sting.

"Well, I *am* good. Want to have a game?"

"Ha! I'd beat you in two minutes flat. I'm probably an expert compared to you."

Okay, so I had two children with big egos.

"Let's do it." Marie lifted her chin in challenge.

"I would, but I have to study." He flashed her a smile that showed a lot of white teeth. "You'll have to lose to me another time."

"You mean *you'll* have to lose."

Brody shrugged. "Whatever." He grabbed a bag of chips from the cupboard just as the doorbell rang. "That's Brent. We'll be downstairs studying."

"For the AP exam—still?" Marie asked.

"Yeah, the AP exam. I want to pass with as many credits as possible. More college credit now means fewer years in college after my mission and the sooner I can get a job and make big bucks."

"Then maybe you can buy me a car."

Brody snorted and went to let Brent in.

Marie rolled her eyes and turned back to us. Dean gave me a brief kiss on the mouth and arose from the couch. "I'm going in to work for a bit," he announced. In an undertone he added, "Call me if you need me."

Marie looked at the two of us as though only now registering that her father was home when he would normally be working. "Your mother isn't feeling well," Dean explained to her unspoken question. He smiled at her, patted her arm, and went out the door. He didn't shut the garage after him, so I got up to shut it. When I'd finished, Marie was still standing absently in the middle of the family room.

"I'll be upstairs if you need me," I said. There was a tinny taste in my mouth, and my stomach was queasy. I worried I might lose the lunch of chicken soup Dean had insisted I eat.

I'd scarcely settled in bed, my scriptures and a novel at my side, when Marie came up to my room.

"Mom?"

"Hi, honey." I patted the bed for her to sit down. She did, pulling one stockinged foot up under her in much the same way I always did. She looked pretty today, with her hair full and slightly curling from the humidity, defying her straightening attempts that morning.

I hoped she didn't want me to take her anywhere. I needed to rest or tomorrow could be much worse, and besides, I didn't feel up to arguing.

"Dad said you're not feeling well," she began.

"I can't take you anywhere, but if you want to go to Becki's—"

"It's weird that you're sick again. You're never sick. Plus, you've been acting kind of funny lately."

I looked into her eyes and saw the worry. Strange that my selfish little Marie should be the one to suspect my sad secret. I'd thought Brody would have questioned me long before she realized anything was amiss. Him or one of my married daughters. But this was the second time Marie had confronted me. She knew I wasn't pregnant from the last confrontation, but she also knew it wasn't like me to spend time in bed—ill or not.

"Well?" she demanded, her voice raising and slightly wobbly.

If I hadn't experienced my epiphany that day, I probably wouldn't have answered, or I would have given her an answer that really wasn't any kind of an answer. But suddenly I knew that to look forward, I needed to tell my children everything. They needed to come to terms with my illness like I was trying to do. They had the right, and even the privilege, of learning and growing along with me. Hiding the truth wasn't helping anyone.

I nodded slowly, those ever-present tears filling my eyes. I inched across the bed, coming closer to my precious little girl who was looking at me with the same concern she'd shown when she was only three and I was down with a severe case of flu. I took her hand. It felt warm and moist in my dry one. At my action, her eyes widened. I wished more than anything that I could protect her from this.

"You're right," I said. "There's something I have to tell you."

Ten

I'd expected Marie to fall into my arms and cry with me, much the way my friend Shirley had when I'd told her. Instead, she pulled her hand from mine and jumped to her feet, her face flushing red and her eyes accusing.

"I can't believe you didn't tell us! What, were you just going to wait until you dropped dead?" Marie burst into tears.

"Honey, no. I wanted to wait until I knew more. I wanted to have better news. I wanted to protect you."

"Stop!" She held up her hand. "I can't—I just can't—" She turned and fled.

I started to follow her, but a bout of nausea made me first pause at the door and then run to my bathroom, where I threw up repeatedly until I was too weak to do anything but slump by the toilet and let tears leak from my eyes.

Moments ticked by, and all I heard was silence. Where was Marie? Should I search for her? I wasn't sure I could make it past my bedroom door, the intense emotions having further depleted my physical energy.

"Mom?" Brody called after what seemed like ages, his voice hoarse and anxious. I knew Marie had told him.

I wiped my mouth with a bit of tissue from the roll. "I'm in here. Just a minute." I flushed the toilet and came into my room. My son was waiting there, looking taller and more gangly than ever—a child, really, not a man. His eyes were frightened, and he looked ready to cry.

"Marie came downstairs. She said . . . Is it true?"

I nodded and started for the bed. He rushed to my side and supported me. His touch was light as though he feared at any moment he would bruise or hurt me.

"Mom," he said as we sat. It was a plea for me to take it away, a plea to look behind us. But we couldn't do that anymore.

"I'm sorry. I should have told you sooner. I didn't want to mess things up."

He hugged me. Gone was the light touch as he searched for comfort like a little boy, holding me so tightly his grip crushed my ribs. His body convulsed with a sob.

"Shush," I said. "It's going to be okay."

I longed to hold my daughter as well, but she hadn't returned. I wondered if she was with Brody's friend Brent downstairs.

"We were looking on the Internet." Tears rolled down Brody's cheeks unchecked. "And it doesn't look like it's going to be okay."

"I'm taking treatments. We'll make the best of it."

"I don't want you to . . ." His words trailed off, filled in by sobs.

"I know. But we'll get through this."

I could see he didn't believe me, this child born of the information age. He'd gone to the Internet to educate himself. Yes, he knew about facts and figures, but he didn't know a thing about tents and angels. I had the responsibility to teach him—and the privilege.

"Look," I said, lying back on my pillows and pulling his head to my shoulder as I'd done when he was a little boy. "I have a story to tell you. It's about Abraham's nephew, Lot, and how he pitched his tent toward Sodom, even though he knew it was a wicked city. It started on a clear, hot day, when the sky was so blue that the beauty of it almost hurt your eyes. Sand stretched for miles—all you could see was sand. And sometimes the wind threw it in your eyes and they would sting."

Brody stilled in my arms, listening to my words. He was always willing to learn now that he was older. I wished Marie would listen.

"It sounds real," he interrupted after a while. "Like you've been there."

I had. I'd been to my own Sodom but was freed by two lovely human angels. "The scriptures come alive," I told him, "if you really try. They can teach you what you need to know here and now. Listen, I'll tell you what they taught me."

It wasn't as easy as I'd hoped to communicate the events I'd experienced, though I did the best I could.

When I was finished explaining, Brody lifted his head. "So you're saying if we're angry about the cancer and if we don't want to accept what the Lord's given us, then we're looking back?" His voice was low but filled with bitterness and disbelief.

I didn't want to minimize his pain. After all, it had taken me six weeks to come this far, and I still didn't accept it all. Or understand how the other scriptures I'd experienced tied in, or what my role was supposed to be. "It's understandable to be upset—angry, even—but if that anger paralyzes us and doesn't allow us to progress, if it eats us up inside so we can't learn from the experience and find some joy, if all we're doing is longing for the past, then we're letting it control us. And that's not good, is it?"

Brody's jaw clenched and unclenched. "I feel really mad," he admitted. "It's not fair."

I tightened my arm around his shoulders and tried to keep my response calm—a hard thing to do when a part of me still cried out at the unfairness. "We've always known that we were put here to learn and to prove ourselves. What good does it do us if we give up when things get tough?"

"That doesn't make it any easier."

"Yes," I said, "it does. Believe me, I know." Before the illness, life had been simple. After, it became a real test. Proving myself now would forever show who I really was—or perhaps who I was becoming.

"I still don't want to do this." My son's voice was a

whisper, and tears threatened to spill from his reddened eyes.

"I know." Truthfully, I didn't know how I could do it, though somehow I would. But how could I help my son? He meant more to me than any bit of life I had left.

"How can I help you?" Brody asked, beating me to the question.

I smiled, wishing I had an answer for both of us. "Just keep being yourself. Keep working at your goals. Keep being an example to Marie."

He looked disappointed, and I knew it wasn't enough. I shifted my position, trying to buy time. My hand fell on the scriptures.

"There is something you could do," I said in a burst of inspiration. "You can help me find a way to pitch my tent toward the Lord. Pitching our tent toward the Lord will make it easier not to look back. I'm not sure exactly how to go about doing it, but I'm sure the answers are in here"—I lifted my scriptures—"if we knew where to look."

His brow creased as he considered my request. Then he nodded, and I knew it was what he'd needed: a puzzle, something to research and resolve.

I let a few heartbeats pass between us before I asked softly, "Where's Marie? Do you know?"

He shook his head. "She left right after we read the stuff on the Internet. She was upset. I told her to come up here with me, but she ran outside. Brent was there. I could go find her."

"Maybe we should give her a little time. It's been a shock. She'll come around."

"What if she does something stupid?"

I understood completely. Too often when Marie was upset, she acted before she thought, and now I had a vision of her running across a road and being hit by a car. Of her going to Becki's and driving somewhere with one of Becki's questionable boyfriends. Perhaps making a terrible mistake that would affect her entire future.

No. I thought. *We are not looking back. I refuse to dwell on the bad.*

I remembered Alma and the power of prayer. We would pray for her now. Taking my son's hand, I looked into his eyes. "Don't worry. An angel will be there for her. An angel who will keep her safe and bring her home."

Eleven

Marie wasn't the only one who ran away. The day after my mother's funeral, I had also left home. Strangely, running away was what saved me.

After my mother died, I had gone a little crazy. I had driven too fast, had run with the wrong crowd. I'd even tried alcohol. My father drank a little himself in the past, so I justified my actions, though I knew my mother would have been horrified.

My father, seeped in his grief over the light that had gone out in our lives, was too blind to notice anything I did. Where before he was always the one to call me down from my room so we could get to church on time, after the accident, neither of us got out of bed. I knew then it had really been my mother who had made us both go. Without her, we didn't care.

My older sister once told me that my father had changed his ways to marry my mother. She'd been engaged to a returned missionary, but she'd fallen in love with my dad instead, and he'd come back to church so she would marry him. Their life together had been happy, but not easy, with his tendency to drink and her struggle with depression. Or maybe one caused the other. But which one? I only knew my father hadn't touched a drop in years before my mother died, but she had still suffered from depression.

I got the alcohol from my mother's things. She had been a wedding planner, and sometimes people gifted her with wine. She always threw it away, without bringing it home where it might tempt my father, but this bottle was buried in a box in the basement, long forgotten. I'd gone there to be close to her, but all I found were sample books filled with invitations, color swatches, menus, and a million other bits of wedding paraphernalia. There was nothing of my mother there, though she had spent much time with couples, poring over those same samples.

Sometimes after she'd helped people, she would come home and stare absently at the books by herself. "What's wrong?" I'd ask, worried that this would signal an onset of an emotional crash.

She'd shake her head. "They're all wrong for each other. It's not going to last."

I never knew her to be wrong, but I hated every time she was right because hearing about one of the marriages failing always caused her to sink into depression. Once I'd asked her why, but she'd only replied, "They said I'd regret marrying your father, that we wouldn't make it, but we're still together. I love your father very much."

If marriage was a struggle for them, life was a struggle for my mother, but they were making it, and they were mostly happy. If it hadn't been for the imbalance in her system and the dreadful mistake that day, I had no doubt they would still be together.

On the day I ran away, my sister, long married and gone from our house, had come to check up on me since my father wasn't doing much of that, and she found me in the basement drinking right from the bottle. She took the wine and dumped it down the drain. Though I begged her not to, she went to call my dad, and when I threatened to leave, she confiscated my car keys.

Furious, I slammed out of the house, vowing to never return.

Unfortunately—or perhaps fortunately—I left my purse and had no money or clothes except those I was wearing. It was late March and still freezing at night, though the days were mild. After staying in the nearby park an hour, I went to one of my friend's houses. She wasn't home, and my other friends lived too far away to get there on foot. I didn't know what to do. I didn't want to go home. I was furious with my family, especially with my mother, who had left me. They said it was an accident, but I told myself she'd really done it on purpose.

I saw the church building. A man emerged from the doors, carrying a large box, and I managed to slip inside before he returned to lock the doors. I decided to hide until later, when I'd sneak home after my dad was sure to be asleep.

As if he would sleep with me missing.

I dozed in a corner of a classroom, and before I knew it, everything was dark and my stomach was growling. I curled up in a ball and cried. I felt stupid then. Everything I'd done was stupid.

I jumped to my feet and ran outside, still not knowing what to do. The door shut behind me, and I was locked out, shivering in the cold.

"Angela?" A flashlight fell over my face, and before I could identify the voice, I was being hugged by a woman. She was my next-door neighbor, Sister Coltrin, the lady who had constantly complained to my parents about how fast I drove, always afraid I'd hit one of her many snotty kids.

I cried on her shoulder, shaking and feeling so much relief. She was a mom. She'd know what to do.

"Look at you! You're shivering." She put her coat on me, but nothing felt as good as her hug. "Come on, let's get to my car. It's warmer there. We need to get you home. The whole neighborhood and the police department are out looking for you. We've all been worried. Especially your dad."

"He's going to kill me."

"Why? Because you drank? Well, probably. But he still loves you. And you'll never do it again, will you?" Her dark eyes pierced me, and I had no choice but to shake my head.

We were quiet for a long time, and then she said, "I'm sorry, Angela. I'm really sorry about everything. I should have been a better neighbor. I'm going to be one now. You mark my words."

For the next year a Sunday never went by without Sister Coltrin coming to get me for church. She'd come a half hour early and wait for me, and no matter how I raged, my dad made me go with her. She'd also send her children to get me for Young Women, and I had to carpool with them to school since dad sold the car I'd been using, presumably to get a better one that never appeared until eighteen months later. By the time I started my senior year, Dad had returned to church, I was president of the Laurel class, and I was driving to school again, even picking up Sister Coltrin's younger children at the junior high afterward. Along with my grandmother and sister, Sister Coltrin was with me in the temple when I took out my endowments and was married.

How wrong I'd been to think the Lord had left me alone. I'd had so much, really. My father, my sister, my friends, scriptures that taught sacred truths, and my beautiful neighbor, who was still out there somewhere, likely being an angel to some other wayward soul. Sister Coltrin hadn't been perfect, had even been a little late, but in the end she'd been faithful and determined.

She'd been an angel. My angel.

Twelve

Marie's angel was Brent. He'd followed her when she ran from our house and taken her to his house, where his mother had plied her with chocolate chip cookies and sympathy—and perhaps a little chastisement, for when Marie came home she was subdued. We were all in the family room watching TV, Dean and I curled up together on the couch and Brody in my chair.

"I'm sorry if I worried you," she said, her eyes rimmed in red and her cheeks spotted with rashes left from her tears.

Brody rolled his eyes. "Duh, Brent called. We weren't worried for long."

Marie smiled. "How sweet of him."

Dean and I looked at each other, struggling not to smile. Though Brent was nice-looking under the glasses, especially now that his face was clearing up, Marie had made no secret of the fact that she thought he was a nerd.

Brody opened his mouth to speak, but I shook my head. Brent was a good crush for Marie. I trusted him more than any of the boys Marie had calling all the time. He'd be going on his mission in a year, so he was safe—more a big brother than anything else. And if she wrote to him and it became something more down the road, well, I wouldn't object.

· · ● · ·

For the next two days I remained flat in bed, pain wracking my body to the point where I wondered if the chemo would kill me before the cancer did. The pain made me question all the resolutions I'd made and brought me back to the brink of despair.

Yet I wasn't alone during my suffering. Dean took both mornings off and worked late instead. He brought me banana sandwiches, cut in triangles, and warm milk in a mug. Brody came home while I was eating and sat with me. He'd all but finished the college classes he was taking through distance learning at the high school, so his schedule was now wide open in the afternoon. Marie's watch began after school was over. She did her math at the kitchen table and then read to me from *The Hiding Place*. I'd read the book in high school and had bought it to read to Marie, but she hadn't wanted to—until now.

I listened to her expressive voice, enjoying every precious moment. Strange how when death spoke everyone listened, and everyone tried to do their best.

Please let me live, I prayed. *Please let me be here for her.* I took a breath before forcing myself to add the rest.

If it be Thy will. I had decided this was part of the key to pitching my tent toward the Lord—accepting His will to be what was best for all of us, for our growth and progression. That didn't mean I couldn't pray for a miracle, a miracle like Sarah and Abraham had experienced, but it meant I needed to continue in faith even if the miracle I wanted didn't materialize. Despite my recent vivid experiences with the scriptures, that was difficult on a day like today.

On the other hand, if it was the Lord's will, I might still be healed like Betty Jones, who was probably living it up in Houston by now, rocking her grandchildren, dancing with widowers, and planning a long summer at the pool.

That sounded a lot better than chemo and radiation.

. . . . .

Our older children responded in various ways to my announcement. My two boys and daughter who lived out of state made plans to visit in the summer. My other two daughters called every day. Sharon, who had always been the closest, both in proximity and emotion, came to my chemo appointments and asked to drive me to receive the radiation as well so Dean wouldn't have to spend so much time away from work.

Marie, however, became my biggest help, though she was often red-eyed and weepy. She learned to do laundry—which she'd never been able to do before despite her A average and honors classes—she did her chores better, and she made dinner a few times each week.

The best thing was that since she now spent more time with her new friend Alison instead of Becki, I was less worried about her, though we sometimes still clashed over what she was allowed to do. Mostly, she would give in, looking at me with wide, frightened eyes, afraid that too much rebellion on her part could kill me on the spot. I might have found it amusing if it hadn't been so close to the truth.

It was the uncertainty, I think, that hurt us most.

Brody took the job I'd given him of finding scriptures very seriously. He was coming to me every day with one scripture or another, and each time I felt strengthened, even when the scripture didn't really seem to apply.

"Look, Mom," he said to me after my fourth chemo treatment, the last before beginning radiation. It had been a difficult week for me, and I'd been struggling to keep positive, to stave off bitterness and depression. Sometimes a nearly insurmountable task.

He placed his scriptures on my lap and settled on the floor next to where I was curled up in my favorite chair. The book was open to Mosiah 24, where the priests of Noah had enslaved and were persecuting the people of Alma, even to the point of threatening death to those who prayed to God. So instead, the people prayed in their hearts, their faith unwavering.

I sat before a loom, weaving a cloth that was far brighter and more intricate than the simple flax tunic I was wearing.

I knew instinctively that this cloth was meant for one of the priests of Noah and not for my own family. My arms were tired, and my leg ached where the guard had whipped me earlier when I had taken too long at the noon meal.

Beyond the covered pavilion where I worked with several women, I could see others in the field, also dressed simply, their backs bending as they worked. I was glad the weather was temperate and that at least they wouldn't die of heat exhaustion. Every now and then, I saw an overseer use his whip and speak with an angry voice. The work went on unceasingly.

Before the loom next to mine sat a tired young woman, her belly large with child. Her face was familiar, but I couldn't place her in my memory. She looked up toward the leaves that covered our open pavilion, and I knew she was praying. I glanced at the guard to make sure he wouldn't see, and when I looked back, the woman was smiling, the exhaustion tucked away out of sight.

I followed her example, praying for strength, and suddenly I did feel stronger, my arms able to carry on their work.

"And now it came to pass that the burdens which were laid upon Alma and his brethren were made light; yea, the Lord did strengthen them that they could bear up their burdens with ease, and they did submit cheerfully and with patience to all the will of the Lord."

Hadn't I felt that exact thing in my own life when I laid my will at the feet of the Lord? But how did this help pitch my tent toward the Lord?

Brody came into the pavilion, carrying a water jug that should have been far too heavy for him, yet he lifted it with ease. He gave drink first to the guard and then to the working women. He handed me the ceramic dish, and I looked into his face.

"See?" Brody said, rising to his knees. "The Lord didn't take away their burdens immediately. He tested them, and then He made their burdens light, or rather, as my seminary teacher says, He made them strong enough to carry their burdens."

Marie was at the table in the kitchen, her pencil poised over her math. I could tell by her stillness that she was listening to what Brody was saying.

"It's true," I said. "I never thought I would be strong enough to go through this. I never thought I could stop looking back. I never thought I'd be able to tell you kids. But I did all that. I was made strong enough for that."

"I never thought Marie would make dinner without burning it." Brody raised his voice to be sure Marie heard. A crumpled paper came flying at his head.

"Let's see if He made your head any stronger," she retorted, popping to her feet. The paper was followed by the lid to her calculator, which solidly hit Brody's head.

He grinned and threw it back. Next went his wallet, and Marie removed the money before lobbing it toward Brody's chest. I laughed.

After a few more moments of horseplay, Marie came to stand next to my chair. "Mom," she said, all traces of teasing gone from her face, "what if I don't want to be strong? Sometimes I think I'd rather be weak. It's easier."

I motioned for her to sit on the edge of the chair and pulled her closer after she did. "Me too," I said, thinking again of the story of Lot and his wife, "but we can't look back. We have to accept our burdens. The Lord is teaching us something. Would you rather tell Him we don't want what He's offering?"

Her face crumpled. "Sort of."

I knew exactly how she felt. But Brody and his scripture had saved me from wanting to give up—at least for today.

Brody put his hand on his sister's shoulder. "Don't worry, Marie. I can carry your burdens until you're strong enough."

She looked at him, her forehead gathered with her frown. "I don't think you can."

"Sure I can. Beginning with that huge math book. You really don't need that, do you? It weighs a ton. Let me help you with that burden by tossing it into the garbage."

They were off again, giggling and teasing, and I knew Brody was right. We *could* help each other with our burdens, maybe even rotating whose turn it was to be strong. Today Brody had helped me endure, to climb back on the path the Lord had shown me. Marie might have needed my reassurance today, but tomorrow she would read to me and be my strength.

That is the power of a family buoyed by a loving God.

Thirteen

I began daily radiation treatments in mid-May, by which time I'd lost another fifteen pounds. The radiation burned my skin and caused me pain and itching, despite the expensive ointment they gave me to smear over the area.

We were doing well, or so I thought, but I spent many hours sitting in bed or throwing up, since I was still having chemo on some Saturdays. Dean was my rock, and I have to admit that I used him all too often, crying out my pain and frustration. I understood now why Betty Jones had said she wasn't going to do chemo again even if her cancer returned. There were moments when the pain was so intense that death seemed a welcome relief, a blissful, magical oblivion where pain wasn't allowed to exist. At those moments—torturously long for all their briefness—I might have even prayed to die if I hadn't so badly wanted to live for Marie and Brody. And, yes, for Dean too.

I should have known that it was too much for my husband—for anyone—to always be the strong one, bearing the family burden when someone else couldn't push the load.

After two weeks of radiation, Dean stood up in church in the middle of a talk and left the rest of us sitting there. I followed him out the door, my children's gazes digging into my back. I knew their concern. Dean had never left church before, and certainly not in the middle of a talk.

I had to move slowly because I never felt well these days, even on my weekends without chemo. By the time I was at the glass doors leading outside, he had slid behind the wheel. I went to the passenger side.

"What is it?" I asked.

"Miracles, miracles! They all get 'em. Why not us?" Bitterness twisted his voice, and if I hadn't been looking right at him, I wouldn't have believed my husband was the man speaking.

For a moment I felt dizzy, as though my life had turned back the clock to more than eight weeks ago when I had been the one to leave church and race down the freeway searching for a solution. How was it some people deserved a miracle and we didn't?

There was still no real answer. Why would God save the life of our neighbor who'd experienced a heart attack, and not save me? Though I held precious hope, I didn't fool myself about my outlook. Even if these treatments were successful enough to allow the surgery, my chances weren't good.

"We've been blessed," I pointed out. "We have our

angels. Look at Shirley, at Brent. Even Marie's new friend. The whole ward has been supportive. The kids are coming in August and bringing the grandchildren. These are angels, Dean. Our angels."

He took my hands. "It's not enough. I want a full miracle. I want you to be healed."

"So do I." Without his support, I felt adrift again, back in the endless sand surrounding the city of Sodom.

There was a knock on the window, and we both looked up to see Brody staring through the window, his unruly hair waving like the wind-swept sand I'd so recently trudged through in my experience with the scriptures. Dean motioned for him to get in the backseat.

Brody had his scriptures with him. "I got it, Mom!" he exclaimed. "It's in Mosiah."

"Got what?" Dean's voice sounded normal now, and I was glad Brody had come. Dealing with my husband's grief was much worse than dealing with my own. I understood now in a way I hadn't before that it was as hard to watch someone you loved die as to be the one dying. Maybe harder.

"It's the words of the prophets. That's what it means to set your tent toward the Lord."

I relaxed. Coming up with these scriptures did him more good than they did me, and I was grateful.

We sat in the doorway of a tent made of animal skins. Beyond the doorway we could see many similar tents and other quickly built structures of wood, some with boughs for a roof, others with fabric coverings. All of the openings faced toward the sacred temple of the Lord.

Near the temple, King Benjamin stood on a wooden structure that towered above the gathering. The hot sun presided over the lush landscape. Beyond the tents were the forests full of vegetation and colorful birds, whose calls occasionally rang out over the noise of the people. The sweet aroma of fruits filled the air.

"My brethren, all ye that have assembled yourselves together, you that can hear my words which I shall speak unto you this day . . . open your ears that ye may hear, and your hearts that ye may understand, and your minds that the mysteries of God may be unfolded to your view."

King Benjamin, not only a king but also a prophet of the Lord. Joy swelled my heart, and tears came to my eyes. How grateful I was for a loving Father who had sent a good man to lead and guide us! Hadn't my family and I gathered together often to hear the prophet of the Lord—our faces, our thoughts, our tents facing him? Yes, we would sit in a modern living room, watching the current prophet on television, instead of in a tent beneath a tower, but I knew it was the same.

I understood now. Setting my tent toward the Lord meant setting it toward the prophet. How much could Lot have benefited from setting his tent toward his prophet instead of the wicked city of Sodom! If he had, his wife would not have looked back.

Joy filled my heart as I watched King Benjamin address his people. I could look forward like they were doing. I could pitch my tent toward the Lord by following the living prophet.

"Mom?" Brody asked eagerly. "Do you see? The people came from all over and faced their tents toward King Benjamin so they could hear what the Lord wanted them to do—you know, the commandments." He beamed, looking younger than his eighteen years.

"Listening to the prophet," I mused aloud. I was proud of him. This was the most relevant scripture he'd come up with so far.

"Well, not just the prophet. It means to hear the words of the Lord—wherever they can be found." He looked at me and then at Dean and back again, his eyes intense, the lines of his face full of awkward angles not yet softened by age. "And what I want to know is, how can you do that here in the car?"

I met Dean's gaze for a long, silent moment, and then without a word he went around the car, opened my door, and helped me out. Hand-in-hand, we went back inside the church, Brody trailing behind.

As we entered the foyer, we saw Evelyn, a woman who lived around the block from us, with her seven-year-old, Stevie. Some less believing would call their presence coincidence. Some would call it fate. I believe it was an answer to prayer. Whose, I don't know. Maybe Brody's or Dean's. Maybe even mine.

Evelyn didn't glance our way. She was poised over Stevie's body in his wheelchair, pushing down on his tiny chest with a vigor that to my unpracticed eye seemed to be dangerously close to crushing him. The boy wheezed. Evelyn pushed down again, her arms like sturdy branches, leaning farther over Stevie to put her weight into the effort. Whenever she paused, the boy coughed and wheezed.

Dean and I stared in fascination. Down Evelyn pushed again, her round, childlike face red with exertion.

"Thanks, Mom," Stevie rasped.

"You feel better?" Evelyn took her hands from his chest and stroked his head that looked impossibly large compared to his toddler-sized body.

"Yes, but the air is funny."

Evelyn adjusted the air tubes going inside his nose. That was new. He'd only had the oxygen tank for the past few weeks, and I knew it couldn't possibly be a good sign. A knot tied itself in my stomach.

Stevie nodded. "Yeah, better." He took a deep breath to prove it, but even I could hear the rattle in his chest from across the room. Stevie had muscular dystrophy, diagnosed when he was only ten months. Slowly but surely he was dying. His muscle, what little he had, would deteriorate to the point that he wouldn't be able to breathe at all—no matter how often or how long his mother pushed on his chest—or his weakened body would succumb to an illness that wouldn't even slow a healthy person down.

I was rooted to the spot. I didn't know Evelyn well, as Stevie was her oldest and her other children too young to move in the same circles as my own. That's often how it went, women becoming friends because of their children, especially in a ward as large and varied as ours.

"Is he okay?" Dean approached Evelyn, the grieving expression back on his face. "Can I help?"

Evelyn smiled and shook her head. "Things build up inside, and we have to get them loose."

"Mom, can I go?" Stevie put his emaciated hand on the controls to his motorized wheelchair.

Evelyn grinned at him. "Oh, so you're feeling strong now, huh? Go ahead, try."

Stevie fumbled with the controls with great effort. This, too, was new. Even as recent as Christmas, Stevie had been able to work his controls with great skill.

Stevie managed to go a few yards down the hallway where Brody was waiting for us so we could go inside together. Evelyn started to go after her son but stopped when Stevie and Brody began talking.

Dean shook his head and muttered, "It's not fair. It's just not fair."

I wasn't sure if Evelyn had heard. She smiled again at me, her eyes luminous. "How are you doing?" It was the kind of pointed question I usually answered by glossing over the facts.

"I don't know," I said. "It's too early to tell."

"I'm sorry."

"I'm sorry too." I looked at Stevie, who was grinning up at Brody, both too far away to hear.

Beside us, Dean clenched and unclenched his fists, ready to bolt or to explode—maybe both. I put my hand on his arm. "Honey, let's go back in."

"What's the point? This is where the real miracle is needed, not in there." He turned to Evelyn. "How can you stand it?"

Emotion filled Evelyn's round face. She looked down at hands that had so recently pumped on her son's chest, essentially extending his life. Her short brown hair fell into her eyes. I wondered if she was going to collapse into tears.

Taking a long breath, she looked up at us, her jaw firm, her eyes steady. "I've had a lot of years to think about it, and what I've come to is this: many people who see miracles are so often like the Nephites, forgetting the Lord as soon as the miracle is behind them. Someday they'll need to be reminded again and even again. Maybe they'll fall away when they don't get what they want. I might have been that way too. Having Stevie in my life makes me remember where I came from and where I want to end up. *He* is the miracle. I'm not about to forget him on any day—or the Lord because of him. I will never stop trying or fall away from the Church because I know the only way I can be with my sweet boy forever is to keep holding onto the gospel and God's promises. My reliance on the Lord is the only reason I survive each day."

I saw it all clearly as she spoke. Scenes from the scriptures where the blind, the lame, the critically ill, all reached out to the Savior to be healed—followed by His loving response. In this age we don't have the opportunity to touch the hem of His robe for a cure, but terminal illness, or extended illness of any type, does keep people from forgetting the Lord. It reminds them daily of their dependence upon Him and brings their understanding of gospel precepts to a new level. How better to appreciate the eternal nature of the family than when one member faces death? How much more likely is a person to search the scriptures when she has a compelling reason to understand the truth? I knew from my own experience that the gospel had become more important in my life than anything else. More important than jobs or houses or cars or vacation or my dream of a restaurant.

Tears dripped from Dean's eyes. I took Evelyn's hand, unable to speak. She was right. Stevie was the miracle—my miracle. And his mother was one more angel sent to help me and my family along this path we had to walk.

Neither Dean nor I could forget the Lord now. Like Evelyn, we needed Him to get through each day. But what if I was actually cured? Would we forget the miracle that would have surely been ours? *No*, I thought, *I won't let that happen. If I'm healed.*

If.

"He's a smart kid," Brody said to us when at last we joined him.

We turned to watch Evelyn help her son hold down the controls to his chair.

"Yes," Dean replied, "he gets it from his mother."

Fourteen

My skin draped on my body, and my hair was thin to the point of having to cut it short and wear a hat, but I felt better than I'd felt in weeks. I'd had my last chemotherapy and radiation treatments at the end of June, and now, a week later, I waited in the hospital to see if the growth had pulled away enough from the artery for me to have the surgery.

The moment of truth.

Dean sat with me, holding my hand. I swallowed hard, difficult because of the sores in my mouth caused by the chemo. They'd heal, I knew, but they made eating even more difficult for me. Not good since Dr. Snell had threatened to put me in the hospital on an IV if I lost more weight.

"Mom?"

I looked up to see Sharon, her stomach finally show-ing her pregnancy. "Honey!" I stood and wrapped my arms around her.

"Brody and Marie told me where you were. Why didn't you tell me?"

"Your father is here." I'd purposely not wanted the children around when we found out if there was a chance for the surgery. I wanted time to prepare if it was bad news.

"Oh, Mom. We should all be here. At least those of us who can." Sharon turned to hug Dean. Father and daughter looked alike, except what was plain on him became pretty in her feminine version. Her dark blonde hair was long and thick, and her eyes held the same unmistakable kindness as her father's.

"Besides, I have news," she added, turning back to me. "I couldn't wait to tell you. It's a girl!"

We squealed and hugged each other again. "Finally, a granddaughter," I said, smiling so hard my face hurt. For that moment I forgot everything else in my joy.

That was when I spied Marie and Brody across the room and waved them over.

"I told you she wouldn't be mad," Sharon said. "We should all be here."

I hugged Brody and Marie. Afterward, we sat waiting, Marie and Dean gripping my hands.

I held my breath when Dr. Snell called Dean and me to his office for consultation. He'd been reluctant to talk during the ultrasound examination, saying he wanted to verify his findings first, and I worried that his reaction meant the worst.

"He's never been one to give false hope," Dean told me. "Let's take him at his word and believe that he really did want to confirm his opinion."

"Well," Dr. Snell began, "I've talked to the radiologist and two other specialists to verify my diagnosis." He grinned, something I had never seen him do before, and it transformed his smallish, tight-looking face. He looked younger and lighter, though his hair was so dark his face already wore a five o'clock shadow. "The surgery is definitely a go."

"Thank you," Dean whispered, though I wasn't sure if he was speaking to the doctor or saying a prayer. He bent down to give me a hug, and I started crying, but this time my tears were happy. Truthfully, I think I'd steeled myself against the possibility of the worst, and this gift, so unexpected, so precious, was the best I could ever remember receiving.

We were alone only a minute. My children came bounding into the room, brought by the nurse, and they fell into our arms, laughing and crying. Only Brody was a little reserved, though I figured that was because we were being watched by several nurses through the door.

"I knew it!" Marie said.

I almost opened my mouth to tell her we were still at the beginning, that anything could happen, but at the joy in her eyes, I changed my mind. We needed this time to celebrate.

"I can't believe it," I murmured dramatically, clasping my hands to my chest. "It can't be true! I just can't believe it!"

Sudden silence fell as everyone looked at me uncertainly. Even to me, my voice sounded odd, and I could see they wondered if I was becoming hysterical, which I could argue I had every right to do, given what I'd been through so far.

"Angela?" Dean asked, reaching out to me.

I gave him my most brilliant smile. "Yep, I can't believe I'm finally going to have a granddaughter!" I started for the door. "Come on, let's get out of here. I suddenly feel hungry enough to eat a moose."

Unfortunately, I'd probably have to settle for a banana sandwich.

Fifteen

"Marie!" Brody shouted from somewhere on the main level. "Phone. It's that girl, Becki." He said it disapprovingly as I once would have. "And you need to remember to keep the garage door shut."

"I was emptying the garbage in the bathroom," Marie called back.

That was amazing in and of itself. Though her cleaning methods had improved, she still almost always forgot to empty the garbage.

I wondered what Becki wanted, and I geared myself up for a fight. From what Marie said and what I could glean from the talk in the neighborhood, Becki was becoming more and more out of control. I didn't want to forbid Marie to see her, but I didn't exactly want to encourage the relationship, either.

Marie came into my room a short while later, *The Hiding Place* tucked under her arm. "Want me to read to you, Mom?"

I nodded. "What about Becki?"

She shrugged. "She wanted to go hang out at the

mall, but I told her about finding out today about the surgery and that I wanted to stay here with you."

I would have done a tap dance if I'd been able. As it was, I sat up and motioned for her to sit beside me.

"Actually . . ." Marie sat down on the bed and stared at the book in her hands. "The truth is, she told me I should say her mother was going to take us down and stay with us, but it was really her boyfriend."

My hand plucked at the bedspread. "What did you say to that?"

"I told her I didn't want to go. Besides, Alison's coming over later. I told Becki to come too, if she wants. Maybe we can be a good influence on her. I hope she comes."

I nodded, but my heart rebelled at the idea. I didn't want her around to influence my daughter.

"She's really not a bad person, Mom," Marie said, her eyes troubled. "She really does believe in the Church, and she wants to do what's right. I think she's just a little, well, lost right now, what with her mom having another baby and all."

Before I could respond, Marie opened the book and began reading, and I was swept away in the story of how Corrie ten Boom had remained faithful through her trials. Her continuous obedience to the commandments had brought great joy in the face of adversity.

At the beginning of my own journey, I'd questioned the worth of adherence to the commandments. Especially when there seemed to be little hope left. *What good had obeying the commandments done for me?* I'd asked in my car on that deserted freeway exit.

Now I knew what I had been given for keeping the commandments all these years—my husband, my children, a knowledge of the truth and by extension a knowledge of God's deep love. The assurance of eternity.

This illness had given me a completely new perspective. Life really was full of opposites. The more suffering I experienced, the more joy I felt in precious moments that I'd once taken for granted. Time with my children, time to feast on the scriptures, time to know my Savior. Every second counted.

Little things like watching a butterfly, seeing a baby bird peer out of a nest, or breathing in the fresh smell of the cleansing rain on the soil took on the meaning they were meant to have when God first created the world. An email from a grandson made me laugh and smile. Brody's plans to send in his mission papers made me proud. Marie's decision to tell the truth filled me with joy.

Joy.

"Hey, Mom." Brody came in, looking slightly flushed from running up the stairs. "Look, it's a postcard from Houston. Do we know anyone in Houston?"

"No, I don't think—" Then I remembered Betty Jones, the pancreatic cancer patient I'd met at my second chemo appointment, the woman who had helped trigger my understanding of what it meant not to look back like Lot's wife.

I swallowed hard, unsure what to expect. Had her cancer returned? Was she enjoying her family? Technically, if she had succumbed, that meant I had that much more of a statistical chance of being the one to survive. But the reality was that we weren't even competing in the same race. Each race, each struggle for life belonged to the individual patient. So far all the pancreatic patients I'd met were at the beginning of diagnosis, had died, or were receiving palliative care—which meant making them comfortable in the short time they had left. Betty was the only one I knew personally who had walked away.

I said a little prayer in my heart.

"Is everything okay?" Brody's face was drawn and pale. There was a tightness around his mouth and a hardness in his eyes that reminded me of the old Marie.

"Yes. It's from a lady I met, that's all." Suddenly I wondered if he'd read it. If he looked upset because of the contents. I quickly scanned the tiny, flowery script on the back of the card.

Dear Angela,

How thoughtful to leave your address. I hope you are doing well. I feel that you must be since I have such an urge to write to you and have finally found the time. As my daughter is expecting again and having a difficult pregnancy, I have been very busy these past months with my grandchildren. It seems I came at exactly the right time. That is

not all—I've begun dating. Yes, at my age! Silly,
I know, but I am having a lot of fun. Remember,
don't look back. There is no changing the past. We
must go forward doing only the best that we can.

> *Sincerely (and healthily) yours,*
> *Betty Jones*

I was crying with relief before I knew it, and Brody reached for me. "I'm sorry, Mom."

I hugged him. "No, no. It's good news. Look, honey." I shoved the card at him. "This is a woman I met. She has—no, had—pancreatic cancer. She's doing well. She's healed!"

"She is? But I thought—" He stopped, looking more like a guilty five-year-old than a young man soon to leave on a mission.

Bless his Internet-reliant little heart. Despite all his scriptures and his faith and endurance, Brody believed the statistics he'd read on the various websites. Even with the good news about the surgery, he didn't believe I had any chance to survive.

"She's alive. She's dating." I laughed through my tears.

He read the card, and I watched his face regain its color. He threw back his head and laughed.

I knew then that my son had—at least for today day—reached his endurance limit, the point where he could no longer be strong. But the Lord had sent Betty

Jones to lighten his burden. Today Betty was strong. She was his angel.

I was strong today too—strong enough to carry his load. Tomorrow or next month, maybe Brody would be ready to pick it up again, and mine along with his own.

I sat at my loom, too exhausted to move. I wanted to leave this place to be free to do my own will. The cut on my calf sent fire up my leg in an agonizing, endless pain. "Please, Father," I mouthed, "help me."

The woman at the loom beside me cried out. I hurried to her side, casting a frightened glance at the Lamanite guard on the other side of the pavilion, his back toward us. "Is it the baby?" I asked.

"No," she said, though her hand went instinctively to the swell of her stomach. "I am weary. I fear I cannot work."

"Rest when he is not looking," I said. "I will weave with all my might and place my cloth on thy pile. Thou art not alone."

She looked at me, tears shimmering, her head bowing in thanks.

New strength rippled through my weary body, and I returned to weave much faster than before, my own hurts forgotten. I glanced once more at the young woman, and at that moment I knew who she resembled—Becki, my daughter's troubled friend.

Sixteen

I awoke later that week on Saturday morning, stretching, a ray of sun angling through the blinds and into my eyes. I wasn't the only one awake. Dean stood by the window in his pajamas. His hand was on the blinds, but he was looking at me. The expression on his face made me want to cry out and to laugh with joy at the same time. I felt his love and support and worry as though they were tangible things like a hug or the banana sandwiches that had kept me alive over the past months. My angel.

Dropping his hand, he came and slipped into the bed beside me, pulling me into his arms. I lay with my head on his shoulder, feeling for the moment a quiet contentment and a profound gratitude that he was mine forever.

"Did you sleep well?" he asked.

I knew he was really asking how I felt. "Yes, and I feel good. Maybe we'll work on the yard today."

He laughed, knowing that meant he would work and I would supervise from the porch swing. He squeezed me more tightly.

On Monday I would have the surgery. Dr. Snell said I'd lose about forty percent of my pancreas, my entire gallbladder, and the first part of my small intestine, called the duodenum. Part of the vein that carried blood to my liver would be replaced with a vein from my leg. Even if they succeeded in getting out all the cancer, I planned to follow up with more chemotherapy, intravenously and by mouth.

I felt hope again, though that very hope sometimes sliced me to the core of my soul. More than anything I wanted to be here for my children. For Dean. I loved them so incredibly much, and I couldn't imagine them going on without me, though of course they would, if they had to.

I was doing everything the doctor had told me to do. Plus I was exercising—when I felt well enough—eating right, and trying to stay positive.

"We could stay right here in bed all day," Dean suggested.

"Ha, you'd get bored."

"I'll never be bored of holding you."

He began to cry. My angel crying. I wiped his cheeks and kissed him until he had no choice but to smile.

"Angela, I love you."

"I know," I told him. "I love you too. It's going to be okay."

How misguided we were to feel that time was slipping between our fingers when in reality we had all eternity. We had to remember that.

I didn't want to die, but I wasn't afraid of dying, either. Not anymore.

If the surgery didn't go well or if the cancer came back years later, I wouldn't despair, and I wouldn't let my family despair. Instead, I would put my whole trust in my God. He knew me and my situation and would send His earthly angels, and heavenly ones unseen, to support me and especially my family. He would make them strong.

He would send friends, teachers, and loving companions to sustain and guide them as He had when I had become a motherless child. I would look down and pray for them and await our joyous reunion. We had been sealed in the temple of the Most High God, and no one could take that promise from us.

Still enfolded in my husband's arms, I lifted my heart to the heavens. *Thank You*, I prayed, *for this knowledge. I appreciate the opportunity to be closer to Thee and to learn to be strong. I promise not to look back with longing and regret like Lot's wife. I will walk with faith the path You have chosen for me. And I'm so grateful for the blessings You always give me in return.*

In the Bible, Sarah had resigned herself to never having a child, yet she was given a miraculous blessing in the Lord's due time. Her miracle touched millions of lives, including my own. Through her I had come to believe that my own personal miracle would occur in the Lord's due time—though not necessarily in this lifetime.

I planned to live my life to the fullest, however long

I was granted. One year, two, five, twenty, forty, it made little difference in the eternal scheme of things. For I had learned that whatever their circumstances, God always, *always*, sends the gift of angels to His children. These angels come in all sizes, shapes, colors, and gender. They are everywhere in our lives. Some we can see, some we can't, some we only read about, but each brings the love and comfort of God to the hearts of those who most desperately need them.

In the time I had left on this beautiful earth, I still had a part to play in reaching out to others—beginning with Marie's friend Becki. Not that I would abandon my daughter to her, but maybe Becki simply needed an angel to guide her home, as I once had in my youth. Maybe I could help her grow into a beautiful, faithful woman like the one who had sat weaving at the loom. I would help her and any others I could find.

I too would become one of the Lord's angels.

fih

V. G 12-3-12